# THE YOGURT COOKBOOK

by
Shona Crawford Poole
and
Jasper Partington

octopus

# Contents

This edition first published 1980 by
Octopus Books Limited
59 Grosvenor Street, London W.1.

ISBN 0 7064 1310 5

Produced and printed in Hong Kong by
Mandarin Publishers Limited
22a Westlands Road, Quarry Bay

# Weights and Measures

All measurements in this book are given in Metric, Imperial and American.

Measurements in weight in the Imperial and American system are the same. Liquid measurements are different, and the following table shows the equivalents:

## Liquid measurements

1 Imperial pint . . . . . . . . . . . . . . . . . . . . . . . . . .  20 fluid ounces
1 American pint . . . . . . . . . . . . . . . . . . . . . . . .  16 fluid ounces
1 American cup . . . . . . . . . . . . . . . . . . . . . . .  8 fluid ounces

Level spoon measurements are used in all recipes.

## Spoon measurements

1 tablespoon . . . . . . . . . . . . . . . . . . . . . . . . . . .  15 ml
1 teaspoon  . . . . . . . . . . . . . . . . . . . . . . . . . . . .  5 ml

When preparing the recipes in this book, only follow one set of measures – they are not interchangeable.

# INTRODUCTION

Indian yogis, who as long ago as 500 BC mixed yogurt with honey, thought it a food for the gods. For centuries yogurt has been an essential ingredient of simple peasant fare and of the exotic dishes of India, the Middle East and the Balkans.

Factory production and fruit-flavoured varieties introduced in the last 50 years have led to its acceptance and growing popularity in Western Europe and America. But yogurt is more than a snack food, and in the recipes which follow I have adapted traditional dishes and made some new ones. Cooking with yogurt is not a health fad either. Though many of the recipes here are useful for slimmers and people on low-cholesterol diets, they have all been included because they are, quite simply, delicious.

Which brings us to the question, is yogurt a health food? Claims for its healing and health-giving powers have been made for more than two thousand years. At various times it has been believed to prolong life, to cure baldness, skin diseases, gastric and many other complaints. It has even been thought an aphrodisiac. Folk lore and myth still cling to yogurt, and science may yet prove some of it right. What can be said with absolute certainty now is that it is more easily digested than milk and every bit as nutritious.

Most of the fresh milk sold today is pasteurized, a heat treatment used to kill potentially harmful bacteria. Much of the fresh milk sold is also homogenized to distribute the cream evenly throughout the milk so that it does not rise to form a layer at the top of the bottle. Then there is ultra-heat treated milk which will keep for months without refrigeration in unopened cartons. Skimmed milk which has had a large part of the fat content removed is increasingly available, both fresh and ultra-heat treated. All these types of milk are suitable for making yogurt at home.

PIQUANT STUFFED TOMATOES *(page 30)*
AND CHILLED WALNUT AND STILTON SOUFFLÉS *(page 27)*

# MAKING YOGURT

Yogurt is simply milk which has been subjected to a controlled souring process using one of the bacteria occurring naturally in untreated milk, usually *lactobacillus bulgaricus* which is the one generally agreed to produce the best flavour. The bacteria are added to the milk either in the form of a powdered starter available at health food counters, or simpler still, just a spoonful or two of natural, unpasteurized yogurt. The tartness and thickness of the homemade yogurt will depend on the temperature and length of its incubation and on the type of milk used.

Yogurt cultures will not grow at temperatures below 32°C/90°F and are destroyed at temperatures above 46°C/115°F. At between 40°-43°C/105°-110°F your yogurt will grow happily. If you cannot test the temperature with a thermometer then a good guide is to dip your finger into the cooling milk. If you can hold your finger in it to a count of 10, and the milk still feels hot, then it is about right.

An electric yogurt-making machine takes the guessing out of temperature control and very quickly pays for itself. Follow the manufacturer's instructions given with the appliance.

To make yogurt without a machine you just have to keep the mixture of milk and starter warm until it has set. This can be done easily by setting a covered bowl in a warm airing cupboard, or on top of a cooker pilot light or central heating boiler, or by pouring it into a vacuum flask, closing tightly and leaving for about 8 hours. Whichever method you choose the yogurt *must* not be jogged, stirred or otherwise disturbed while it is incubating. If it is, it will separate. Refrigerate yogurt immediately it has set, and preferably for several hours before serving.

10

# Whole Milk Natural (Unflavored) Yogurt

Use this thick, creamy yogurt for any of the recipes in this book. If you are using commercially made yogurt as a starter check that it has not been pasteurized after culturing.

METRIC/IMPERIAL
*1 litre/1 3/4 pints milk*
*1 tablespoon natural yogurt or powdered starter*

AMERICAN
*4 1/4 cups milk*
*1 tablespoon unflavored yogurt or powdered starter*

Heat the milk in a saucepan until almost boiling. Remove it from the heat immediately and set aside until it has cooled to 40–43°C/ 105–110°F. (Use a thermometer for accuracy.) Stir in the yogurt or powdered starter and whisk lightly together.

Pour the mixture into clean jars or bowls, cover and incubate at 40–43°C/105–110°F for 6 to 10 hours, or until firm. Refrigerate for several hours before serving.
**Makes 1 litre/1 3/4 pints/4 1/4 cups**

# Low Fat Natural (Unflavored) Yogurt

Fresh or ultra-heat treated skimmed milk may be used for this recipe. The additional dried milk firms the yogurt which would otherwise be thin and lacking in body.

METRIC/IMPERIAL
*1 litre/1 3/4 pints skimmed milk*
*4 tablespoons powdered skimmed milk*
*1 tablespoon natural yogurt or powdered starter as directed*

AMERICAN
*4 1/4 cups skimmed milk*
*1/4 cup powdered skimmed milk*
*1 tablespoon unflavored yogurt or powdered starter as directed*

Heat the milk in a saucepan until almost boiling. Remove it from the heat immediately and set aside until it has cooled to 40–43°C/ 105–110°F. (Use a thermometer for accuracy.) Stir in the powdered skimmed milk and yogurt or powdered starter and whisk lightly together.

Pour the mixture into jars or bowls, cover and incubate at 40–43°C/105–110°F for 6 to 10 hours, or until firm. Refrigerate for several hours before serving.
**Makes 1 litre/1 3/4 pints/4 1/4 cups**

# Yogurt Curd Cheese

Use whole milk natural (unflavored) yogurt to make this soft curd cheese. Season the cheese with salt and freshly ground black pepper and flavour it with herbs, garlic or chopped spring onions (scallions) to serve as a snack or first course with freshly baked bread, toast or crispbread. Or serve it Arab fashion, salted and formed into balls sprinkled with olive oil and paprika. Whipped with sugar to taste and a little whipped cream, it makes a luxurious dessert topping.

| METRIC/IMPERIAL | AMERICAN |
|---|---|
| 1 litre/1¾ pints whole milk natural yogurt (see page 11) | 4¼ cups whole milk unflavored yogurt (see page 11) |

Line a large sieve (strainer) or colander with a square of damp muslin (cheesecloth) and set it over a bowl. Beat the yogurt and pour it into the lined sieve (strainer). Gather up the corners of the muslin (cheesecloth) and tie them together. Hang the bag of curds over a bowl for about 4 hours, by which time the whey will have dripped out. Longer draining makes a drier, thicker cheese. Refrigerate the yogurt curd cheese and use it within 3 or 4 days.
**Makes about 350 g/12 oz/1½ cups**

# Thickened Yogurt

This is the best kind of yogurt to use for ices. The gelatine in the recipe inhibits the formation of large ice crystals and helps to make really smooth ices.

| METRIC/IMPERIAL | AMERICAN |
|---|---|
| 1 sachet gelatine | 1 sachet unflavored gelatin |
| 1 litre/1¾ pints milk | 4¼ cups milk |
| 1 tablespoon natural yogurt or powdered starter as directed | 1 tablespoon unflavored yogurt or powdered starter as directed |

Sprinkle the gelatine on 150 ml/¼ pint/⅔ cup of the milk, stir and leave for about 5 minutes until soft and swollen.

Heat the remaining milk in a saucepan until almost boiling. Remove it from the heat, stir in the softened gelatine and stir until the gelatine has dissolved completely. Set the milk aside until it has cooled to 40–43°C/105–110°F (use a thermometer for accuracy) then whisk in the yogurt or powdered starter.

Pour the mixture into clean jars or bowls, cover and incubate at 40–43°C/105–110°F for 6 to 10 hours, or until firm. Refrigerate for several hours before serving.
**Makes 1 litre/1¾ pints/4¼ cups**

YOGURT CURD CHEESE SHAPED INTO ROUNDS, FLAVOURED WITH HERBS OR WHIPPED

# Coffee Yogurt

Make with skimmed milk, coffee yogurt is a pleasant dessert for slimmers.

METRIC/IMPERIAL
1 litre/1³/4 pints skimmed milk
4 tablespoons powdered skimmed
  milk
2 tablespoons instant coffee
4 tablespoons sugar
1 tablespoon natural yogurt or
  powdered starter as directed

AMERICAN
4¹/4 cups skimmed milk
¹/4 cup powdered skimmed milk
2 tablespoons instant coffee
¹/4 cup sugar
1 tablespoon unflavored yogurt or
  powdered starter as directed

Heat the milk in a saucepan until almost boiling. Remove it from the heat immediately and set aside until it has cooled to 40–43°C/105–110°F. (Use a thermometer for accuracy.) Stir in the powdered skimmed milk, instant coffee, sugar and yogurt or powdered starter and whisk lightly together.

Pour the mixture into clean jars or bowls, cover and incubate at 40–43°C/105–110°F for 6 to 10 hours, or until firm. Refrigerate for several hours before serving.
**Makes 1 litre/1³/4 pints/4¹/4 cups**

# Vanilla Yogurt

METRIC/IMPERIAL
1 litre/1³/4 pints milk
10 cm/4 inch piece vanilla pod*
100 g/4 oz sugar
1 tablespoon natural yogurt or
  powdered starter as directed

AMERICAN
4¹/4 cups milk
4 inch piece vanilla bean*
¹/2 cup sugar
1 tablespoon unflavored yogurt or
  powdered starter as directed

Heat together slowly the milk and the piece of vanilla split in halves lengthwise. When almost boiling, remove the pan from the heat and set aside until the milk has cooled to 40–43°C/105–110°F. (Use a thermometer for accuracy.) Take out the vanilla. Stir in the sugar and the yogurt or powdered starter and whisk lightly together.

Pour the mixture into clean jars or bowls, cover and incubate at 40–43°C/105–110°F for 6 to 10 hours, or until firm. Refrigerate for several hours before serving.
**Makes 1 litre/1³/4 pints/4¹/4 cups**

*To substitute vanilla essence (extract) add 1 to 2 teaspoons to the cooled milk.

# Goat's Milk Yogurt

METRIC/IMPERIAL
*1 litre/1¾ pints goat's milk*
*powdered starter as directed*

AMERICAN
*4¼ cups goat's milk*
*powdered starter as directed*

Heat the milk to boiling point in a large saucepan and when it rises lower the heat and simmer it very gently for 2 minutes. Remove the milk from the heat and set it aside until it has cooled to 40–43°C/ 105–110°F. (Use a thermometer for accuracy.) Stir in the powdered starter and whisk lightly together.

Pour the mixture into clean jars or bowls, cover, and incubate at 40–43°C/105–110°F for 6 to 10 hours or until firm. Refrigerate for several hours before serving.

**Makes 1 litre/1¾ pints/4¼ cups**

# Stabilized Yogurt

When yogurt is to be used for garnishing hot soups or vegetables it should first be stabilized, otherwise it will curdle when it comes into contact with the hot food. Use this method to stabilize bought or homemade whole milk or low fat yogurt.

METRIC/IMPERIAL
*1 litre/1¾ pints natural yogurt*
*1 tablespoon cornflour*

AMERICAN
*4¼ cups unflavored yogurt*
*1 tablespoon cornstarch*

Tip the yogurt into a saucepan and whisk it until it is liquid. Add the cornflour (cornstarch) and whisk until it is thoroughly blended. Bring slowly to the boil stirring in one direction only. Simmer for 10 minutes, or until thick, then leave uncovered until cool.

Cover and refrigerate until needed. Stabilized yogurt will keep in the refrigerator for up to 2 weeks.

**Makes 1 litre/1¾ pints/4¼ cups**

# Stir-up Fruit Cups

If you make this recipe with skimmed milk add a little dried skimmed milk to give the yogurt extra body.

| METRIC/IMPERIAL | AMERICAN |
| --- | --- |
| 1 litre/1¾ pints milk | 4¼ cups milk |
| 1 tablespoon natural yogurt or powdered starter as directed | 1 tablespoon unflavored yogurt or powdered starter as directed |
| 1-2 tablespoons jam | 1-2 tablespoons jelly |

Heat the milk in a saucepan until it is almost boiling. Remove it from the heat immediately and set aside until it has cooled to 40–43°C/105–110°F. (Use a thermometer for accuracy.) Stir in the yogurt or powdered starter and whisk lightly together.

Spoon 1 or 2 tablespoons of jam (jelly) into the bottom of each of 6 jars or cups and fill them up with the milk mixture. Cover the containers and incubate at 40–43°C/105–110°F for 6 to 10 hours, or until firm. Refrigerate for several hours before serving.
**Serves 6**

# Honey Yogurt Pots

| METRIC/IMPERIAL | AMERICAN |
| --- | --- |
| 1 litre/1¾ pints milk | 4¼ cups milk |
| 4 tablespoons powdered skimmed milk | ¼ cup powdered skimmed milk |
| 120 ml/4 fl oz runny honey | ½ cup runny honey |
| 1 tablespoon natural yogurt or powdered starter as directed | 1 tablespoon unflavored yogurt or powdered starter as directed |

Heat the milk in a saucepan until almost boiling. Remove it from the heat immediately and stir in the powdered milk, then the honey. Set aside until the mixture has cooled to 40–43°C/105–110°F. (Use a thermometer for accuracy.) Stir in the yogurt or powdered starter and whisk lightly together.

Pour the mixture into clean jars or bowls, cover, and incubate at 40–43°C/105–110°F for 6 to 10 hours, or until firm. Refrigerate for several hours before serving.
**Makes 1.2 litres/2 pints/5 cups**

FROM LEFT: HONEY YOGURT POTS; BREAKFAST SHAKE AND HAZELNUT MUESLI YOGURT (both page 19)

# BREAKFASTS

## Sweetcorn Fritters

### METRIC/IMPERIAL
100 g/4 oz plain flour
1 egg
5 tablespoons natural yogurt
5 tablespoons milk
1 x 225 g/8 oz can creamed
  sweetcorn
salt to taste
freshly ground black pepper to taste
50 g/2 oz butter
1 tablespoon vegetable oil

### AMERICAN
1 cup all-purpose flour
1 egg
5 tablespoons unflavored yogurt
5 tablespoons milk
1 x 1/2 lb can creamed sweetcorn
salt to taste
freshly ground black pepper to taste
1/4 cup butter
1 tablespoon vegetable oil

Sift the flour into a bowl and make a well in the middle. Combine the egg, yogurt and milk in another bowl and mix lightly together. Pour the liquid into the flour all at once and draw the flour in gradually, stirring with a wooden spoon to make a smooth batter. Stir in the creamed corn and season to taste with salt and pepper.

Heat the butter and oil together in a large frying pan (skillet) over a medium heat. When hot, drop tablespoons of the batter into the hot fat and cook until the fritters are golden brown on the underside. Flip them over and continue cooking until the other side is golden too.

Drain the fritters on absorbent kitchen paper and keep warm while the remaining batter is fried.

Serve very hot with fried bacon or gammon ham steaks.
**Makes about 8**

# Hazelnut Muesli Yogurt

| METRIC/IMPERIAL | AMERICAN |
|---|---|
| *50 g/2 oz shelled hazelnuts* | *½ cup shelled filberts* |
| *100 g/4 oz muesli* | *1½ cups muesli* |
| *600 ml/1 pint natural yogurt (see page 11)* | *2½ cups unflavored yogurt (see page 11)* |

Spread the hazelnuts (filberts) on a baking sheet and roast them in a preheated moderate oven (160°C/325°F, Gas Mark 3) for about 15 minutes, or until the centres are a pale biscuit (cookie) colour. Cool the nuts, rub off the skins and grind or pound the kernels to the texture of coarse breadcrumbs.

Combine the nuts, muesli and yogurt in a bowl and mix well together. Cover and chill for at least an hour before serving.
**Makes about 900 ml/1½ pints/3¾ cups**

# Breakfast Shake

| METRIC/IMPERIAL | AMERICAN |
|---|---|
| *150 ml/¼ pint natural yogurt (see page 11)* | *⅔ cup unflavored yogurt (see page 11)* |
| *1 egg* | *1 egg* |
| *1 tablespoon wheatgerm* | *1 tablespoon wheatgerm* |
| *1 tablespoon honey* | *1 tablespoon honey* |
| *2 tablespoons concentrated frozen orange juice* | *2 tablespoons concentrated frozen orange juice* |

Tip all the ingredients into a blender goblet and blend for a moment or two until smooth.

Serve immediately in a large tumbler.
**Serves 1**

*Variations:* Substitute grapefruit or pineapple juice, or any soft fruits for orange juice.

# Breakfast Pancakes

METRIC/IMPERIAL
*275 g/10 oz plain flour*
*1 tablespoon caster sugar*
*2 teaspoons cream of tartar*
*1 teaspoon bicarbonate of soda*
*1 teaspoon salt*
*2 large eggs*
*3 tablespoons melted butter or*
  *bacon fat*
*250 ml/8 fl oz natural yogurt (see*
  *page 11)*
*250 ml/8 fl oz milk*

AMERICAN
*2½ cups all-purpose flour*
*1 tablespoon superfine sugar*
*2 teaspoons cream of tartar*
*1 teaspoon baking soda*
*1 teaspoon salt*
*2 large eggs*
*3 tablespoons melted butter or*
  *bacon fat*
*1 cup unflavored yogurt (see*
  *page 11)*
*1 cup milk*

Sift all the dry ingredients into a mixing bowl. In another bowl combine the remaining ingredients and whisk lightly together. Tip the liquid into the flour mixture all at once and beat well to form a thick batter.

Heat a frying pan (skillet) over a medium heat and grease it lightly. To make 2 or 3 pancakes at a time, drop about 4 tablespoons/¼ cup portions of batter into the pan, spacing them well apart. Cook until bubbles appear on the surface of the pancakes, then flip them over to cook on the other side until brown. Continue until all the batter is used up.

Serve the pancakes very hot with grilled (broiled) or fried bacon and fried egg, or with hot syrup.
**Makes about 12**

# Prune and Orange Yogurt

METRIC/IMPERIAL
*1 large orange*
*10 large prunes, stoned*
*2 tablespoons sugar*
*1 litre/1¾ pints thickened yogurt*
  *(see page 12)*

AMERICAN
*1 large orange*
*10 large prunes, pitted*
*2 tablespoons sugar*
*4¼ cups thickened yogurt*
  *(see page 12)*

Finely grate the zest of the orange then squeeze out the juice. Put the zest and juice in a small saucepan with the prunes and sugar and bring to the boil. Remove the pan from the heat, cover and set aside until the prunes are plumped. Purée the prunes in an electric blender or rub them through a sieve (strainer). Combine the prune purée and yogurt and whisk lightly together.

Pour the mixture into 6 or 8 glasses or bowls, cover, and refrigerate for several hours before serving well chilled.
**Serves 6-8**

# APPETIZERS AND DIPS

## Tahina Yogurt Cream

Tahina paste, sold in Greek food shops and many delicatessens and supermarkets, is made from sesame seeds.

METRIC/IMPERIAL
*4 cloves garlic, peeled*
*salt to taste*
*175 ml/6 fl oz tahina paste*
*175 ml/6 fl oz natural yogurt*
*4 tablespoons lemon juice*
*freshly ground black pepper to taste*
*2 tablespoons chopped parsley to garnish*

AMERICAN
*4 cloves garlic, peeled*
*salt to taste*
*3/4 cup tahina paste*
*3/4 cup unflavored yogurt*
*1/4 cup lemon juice*
*freshly ground black pepper to taste*
*2 tablespoons chopped parsley to garnish*

Crush the garlic with a little salt and put it into a bowl with the tahina paste. Gradually beat in the yogurt and lemon juice to make a smooth, creamy mixture. Season to taste with salt and black pepper.

Divide the mixture between 6 individual ramekins or put it all in one bowl. Sprinkle with chopped parsley.

Serve at room temperature or chilled.
**Serves 4-6**

# Salmon Mousse

To make a festive looking dish use a fish-shaped mould for this mousse. Whatever shape of mould you choose, it should hold about 1 litre/1¾ pints/4¼ cups.

| METRIC/IMPERIAL | AMERICAN |
|---|---|
| 1½ sachets gelatine | 1½ sachets unflavored gelatin |
| 175 ml/6 fl oz water | ¾ cup water |
| 300 ml/½ pint yogurt mayonnaise (see page 67) | 1¼ cups yogurt mayonnaise (see page 67) |
| 1 tablespoon finely chopped onion | 1 tablespoon finely chopped onion |
| 1 tablespoon finely chopped fresh dill or fennel | 1 tablespoon finely chopped fresh dill or fennel |
| 1 tablespoon lemon juice | 1 tablespoon lemon juice |
| 500 g/1 lb cooked, fresh salmon, or drained, canned salmon | 1 lb cooked, fresh salmon, or drained, canned salmon |
| salt to taste | salt to taste |
| freshly ground black pepper to taste | freshly ground black pepper to taste |
| **To Garnish:** | **To Garnish:** |
| sliced cucumber or watercress sprigs | sliced cucumber or watercress sprigs |

Sprinkle the gelatine on the water in a small saucepan and when it has swollen, heat until the gelatine has dissolved completely.

In a bowl combine the yogurt mayonnaise, onion, dill or fennel and lemon juice. Add the dissolved gelatine, mix well and set aside until the mixture is just beginning to set.

Remove all the skin and bones from the salmon and flake the flesh. Combine the salmon with the mayonnaise mixture, preferably in an electric blender for a velvety texture, and blend until smooth. Season the mixture generously with salt and freshly ground black pepper.

Turn the mixture into a wetted mould, cover and chill for an hour, or until set.

To unmould the mousse, dip the mould briefly in hot water. Invert a serving plate over the mould, and holding the two together, turn the right way up. Shake gently to release the mousse. Garnish the mousse with sliced cucumber or watercress.
**Serves 6-8**

*Variations:* Substitute smoked mackerel or drained, canned tuna for the salmon.

# Cheese Dip

The flavours of many varieties of cheese go well with yogurt to make any number of different dips. This is a very good way to use up bits of cheese which are still in good condition but are too small to offer on a cheese board. Add chopped onion, chives or other herbs to taste. Serve cheese dips with crisp savoury crackers, or with chunks of raw vegetables like cucumber, carrot, radishes, celery, red or green pepper, spring onions (scallions), and cauliflower.

| METRIC/IMPERIAL | AMERICAN |
|---|---|
| *100 g/4 oz grated cheese* | *1 cup grated cheese* |
| *2 tablespoons natural yogurt* | *2 tablespoons unflavored yogurt* |
| *120 ml/4 fl oz yogurt curd cheese* | *½ cup yogurt curd cheese (see page* |
| *(see page 12) or cream cheese* | *12) or cream cheese* |
| *salt to taste* | *salt to taste* |
| *freshly ground black pepper to taste* | *freshly ground black pepper to taste* |

Put all the ingredients in a bowl and mix well with a fork until smooth. Check the seasoning.

Serve immediately, or, alternatively, cover closely and store in the refrigerator for up to a week, less if you have added raw onion or herbs to the mixture.

**Makes about 350 ml/12 fl oz/1½ cups**

# Marinated Mushrooms

Choose very fresh, tightly closed mushrooms for this recipe.

| METRIC/IMPERIAL | AMERICAN |
|---|---|
| *500 g/1 lb button mushrooms* | *1 lb button mushrooms* |
| *250 ml/8 fl oz natural yogurt* | *1 cup unflavored yogurt* |
| *2 tablespoons olive oil* | *2 tablespoons olive oil* |
| *1 tablespoon lemon juice* | *1 tablespoon lemon juice* |
| *salt to taste* | *salt to taste* |
| *freshly ground black pepper to taste* | *freshly ground black pepper to taste* |

Wipe the mushrooms with a clean cloth and cut off the stalks level with the base of each cap. Reserve the stalks for another recipe. Slice the mushrooms thickly.

Combine all the remaining ingredients and mix well. Add the mushrooms and stir gently in the dressing until the pieces are thoroughly coated. Cover and refrigerate for at least 2 hours before serving.

Serve the marinated mushrooms with plenty of hot, crusty bread.
**Serves 6**

# Tagliatelle with Ham and Mushrooms

METRIC/IMPERIAL
*225 g/8 oz green tagliatelli*
**Sauce:**
*25 g/1 oz butter*
*1 small onion, finely chopped*
*100 g/4 oz button mushrooms*
*100 g/4 oz cooked ham, chopped*
*2 tablespoons flour*
*450 ml/3/4 pint milk*
*150 ml/1/4 pint natural yogurt*
*salt to taste*
*freshly ground black pepper to taste*
*grated nutmeg to taste*
*4-6 tablespoons grated Parmesan*
  *cheese to serve*

AMERICAN
*1/2 lb green tagliatelli*
**Sauce:**
*2 tablespoons butter*
*1 small onion, finely chopped*
*1 cup button mushrooms*
*1/2 cup chopped, cooked cured ham*
*2 tablespoons flour*
*2 cups milk*
*2/3 cup unflavored yogurt*
*salt to taste*
*freshly ground black pepper to taste*
*grated nutmeg to taste*
*4-6 tablespoons grated Parmesan*
  *cheese to serve*

Cook the tagliatelli in plenty of boiling salted water until it is just tender. The length of time it takes to cook will depend on the brand. Start the sauce when you start the tagliatelli, and if the pasta is ready first, drain it in a large sieve (strainer) and turn it into a warm serving bowl. Keep warm.

Melt the butter in a pan and add the onion and mushrooms. Cook gently together until the onion is soft but not brown, then add the ham. Stir over a low heat for a minute or two then sprinkle the flour over the mixture. Gradually add the milk and cook the mixture for a few minutes until it thickens. Just before serving, stir in the yogurt and season the sauce with salt, freshly ground black pepper and grated nutmeg.

As soon as the yogurt is well blended, pour the sauce over the drained tagliatelli and serve immediately. Hand the Parmesan cheese separately.
**Serves 4-6**

*Variations:* Substitute crisp bacon, prawns (shrimp) or tuna fish for the ham.

# Chilled Walnut and Stilton Soufflés

Serve this unusual chilled first course in individual 150 ml/¼ pint/⅔ cup soufflé dishes. Prepare the dishes with collars of greaseproof (wax) paper or foil. Serve with salty crackers or pretzels.

| METRIC/IMPERIAL | AMERICAN |
| --- | --- |
| 25 g/1 oz butter | 2 tablespoons butter |
| 2 tablespoons plain flour | 2 tablespoons all-purpose flour |
| 450 ml/¾ pint natural yogurt | 2 cups unflavored yogurt |
| 100 g/4 oz Stilton cheese, crumbled | 1 cup crumbled Stilton cheese |
| salt to taste | salt to taste |
| freshly ground black pepper to taste | freshly ground black pepper to taste |
| 1 tablespoon gelatine | 1 tablespoon unflavored gelatin |
| 4 tablespoons water | ¼ cup water |
| 50 g/2 oz chopped walnuts | ½ cup chopped walnuts |
| 150 ml/¼ pint double cream | ⅔ cup heavy cream |
| 3 egg whites | 3 egg whites |
| 6 walnut halves to garnish | 6 walnut halves to garnish |

Melt the butter in a saucepan then stir in the flour. Cook the *roux* for a minute or two, then gradually add the yogurt, stirring constantly. Stir in the cheese and cook gently until it has melted. Season to taste with salt and pepper.

Soak the gelatine in the water and add it to the sauce. Stir until it has dissolved completely then set the mixture aside to cool.

When the sauce is cold and just on the point of setting stir in the walnuts. Whip the cream until it holds a peak, and whisk the egg whites in a separate bowl until they hold stiff peaks. Fold the cream and egg whites into the cheese mixture.

Divide the mixture between 6 prepared soufflé dishes and chill for at least an hour.

To serve, carefully remove the collars and top each soufflé with a walnut half.

**Serves 6**

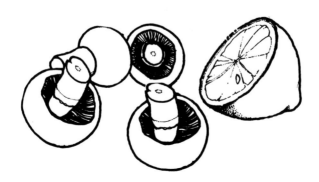

# Artichokes with Yogurt Hollandaise

METRIC/IMPERIAL
*2 tablespoons lemon juice*
*2 tablespoons salt*
*6 globe artichokes*
**Sauce:**
*1 tablespoon lemon juice*
*salt to taste*
*freshly ground black pepper to taste*
*100 g/4 oz softened butter*
*4 egg yolks*
*120 ml/4 fl oz natural yogurt*

AMERICAN
*2 tablespoons lemon juice*
*2 tablespoons salt*
*6 globe artichokes*
**Sauce:**
*1 tablespoon lemon juice*
*salt to taste*
*freshly ground black pepper to taste*
*½ cup softened butter*
*4 egg yolks*
*½ cup unflavored yogurt*

Take a pan, or pans, large enough to hold the artichokes in one layer and fill it, or them, with water to a depth of 10 cm/4 inches. Add the lemon juice and salt and bring to the boil. Break the stalks off the artichokes so that as few as possible of the tough stalk fibres extend into the heart and drop the artichokes into the water. Bring back to the boil, reduce the heat and simmer, covered, for 30 to 50 minutes. The artichokes are ready when a leaf from near the base can be pulled off easily. The cooking time will depend on their size and age.

Drain the artichokes upside down. Wearing rubber gloves to protect your fingers from the heat, spread the leaves away from the middle and pull out the central leaves and hairy choke. Reshape the artichokes and arrange them on a serving platter.

To make the sauce, combine the lemon juice with a little salt and pepper in the top of a double boiler. The water in the bottom pan should be just below boiling point. Add 2 tablespoons of the butter and all the egg yolks and whisk briskly together until the mixture thickens. Whisking constantly, gradually add the remaining butter, followed by the yogurt. Whisk the mixture until the sauce is thick and light, be careful that the water underneath does not boil and cause the sauce to curdle.

Serve immediately with the hot artichokes.

**Serves 6**

# Piquant Stuffed Tomatoes

Choose the big, pumpkin-shaped tomatoes for this recipe. Dried basil does not have mush taste, so if you cannot find fresh basil increase the quantities of chives and parsley.

METRIC/IMPERIAL

6 large, ripe tomatoes
225 g/8 oz yogurt curd cheese (see
  page 12)
1 small onion, peeled and finely
  chopped
2 tablespoons chopped basil
2 tablespoons snipped chives
2 tablespoons chopped parsley
1 tablespoon olive oil
120 ml/4 fl oz double cream
salt to taste
freshly ground black pepper to taste
cayenne pepper to taste
6 sprigs of fresh basil or parsley to
  garnish

AMERICAN

6 large, ripe tomatoes
½ lb yogurt curd cheese (see
  page 12)
1 small onion, peeled and finely
  chopped
2 tablespoons chopped basil
2 tablespoons snipped chives
2 tablespoons chopped parsley
1 tablespoon olive oil
½ cup heavy cream
salt to taste
freshly ground black pepper to taste
cayenne pepper to taste
6 sprigs of fresh basil or parsley to
  garnish

Slice the top off each tomato, and, using a teaspoon, carefully scoop out the seeds and membranes to leave a hollow shell. Invert the shells and lids and leave them to drain while you make the filling.

Put the yogurt curd cheese in a bowl. Add the onion, basil, chives, parsley and oil and mix well.

In a separate bowl beat the cream until it holds stiff peaks. Add the cream to the cheese mixture and beat lightly together. Season to taste with salt, pepper and cayenne.

Fill the drained tomato cups with the cream cheese mixture. Replace the lids and chill well before serving.

Just before serving, top each tomato with a sprig of basil or parsley.
**Serves 6**

# SOUPS

# Vichyssoise

The traditional recipe for this famous American soup is rich in cream. This lighter version, including yogurt, is less expensive and excellent in its own right.

| METRIC/IMPERIAL | AMERICAN |
|---|---|
| *500 g/1 lb leeks* | *1 lb leeks* |
| *250 g/8 oz potatoes* | *½ lb potatoes* |
| *50 g/2 oz butter* | *¼ cup butter* |
| *600 ml/1 pint chicken stock* | *2½ cups chicken stock* |
| *600 ml/1 pint milk* | *2½ cups milk* |
| *250 ml/8 fl oz natural yogurt, beaten until liquid* | *1 cup unflavored yogurt, beaten until liquid* |
| *salt to taste* | *salt to taste* |
| *freshly ground black pepper to taste* | *freshly ground black pepper to taste* |
| **To Garnish:** | **To Garnish:** |
| *150 ml/¼ pint single cream* | *⅔ cup light cream* |
| *2 tablespoons snipped chives* | *2 tablespoons snipped chives* |

Trim the leeks and slit them in halves lengthwise. Wash them thoroughly and chop finely. Peel and dice the potatoes.

Melt the butter in a large saucepan, add the chopped leeks and potatoes and sauté gently together for about 10 minutes without allowing them to brown. Add the chicken stock and milk, bring to the boil, cover and simmer for about 30 minutes. Set aside to cool.

Purée the mixture in a blender or rub it through a sieve (strainer). Add the yogurt, and salt and pepper to taste and mix well. Chill thoroughly.

To serve, pour the cream in a swirl on top of the soup, either in 1 large bowl or individual servings, and scatter with snipped chives.
**Serves 6**

# Avocado Gazpacho

| METRIC/IMPERIAL | AMERICAN |
|---|---|
| 1 litre/1³⁄₄ pints light chicken stock | 4¹⁄₄ cups light chicken stock |
| 1 medium onion, chopped | 1 medium onion, chopped |
| 1 small green pepper, deseeded and chopped | 1 small green pepper, deseeded and chopped |
| ¹⁄₂ cucumber, peeled and chopped | ¹⁄₂ cucumber, peeled and chopped |
| 1 large, ripe avocado, peeled, stoned and chopped | 1 large, ripe avocado, peeled, pitted and chopped |
| 150 ml/¹⁄₄ pint natural yogurt | ²⁄₃ cup unflavored yogurt |
| 1 tablespoon wine vinegar | 1 tablespoon wine vinegar |
| salt to taste | salt to taste |
| freshly ground black pepper to taste | freshly ground black pepper to taste |
| cayenne pepper to taste | cayenne pepper to taste |
| 1 avocado, peeled, stoned and sliced, to garnish | 1 avocado, peeled, pitted and sliced, to garnish |

In a blender goblet combine the stock with the chopped onion, green pepper, cucumber, avocado, yogurt and vinegar and blend until smooth. Season to taste with salt, pepper and cayenne. Pour the soup into a serving dish and chill well.

Just before serving prepare the avocado garnish and float the slices of avocado on the soup.

**Serves 6**

# Chilled Tomato Soup

| METRIC/IMPERIAL | AMERICAN |
|---|---|
| 1 kg/2 lb ripe tomatoes | 2 lb ripe tomatoes |
| 300 ml/¹⁄₂ pint natural yogurt | 1¹⁄₄ cups unflavored yogurt |
| 4 tablespoons lemon juice | ¹⁄₄ cup lemon juice |
| 2 tablespoons olive oil | 2 tablespoons olive oil |
| 1 tablespoon fresh thyme leaves, or 1 teaspoon dried thyme | 1 tablespoon fresh thyme leaves, or 1 teaspoon dried thyme |
| salt to taste | salt to taste |
| freshly ground black pepper to taste | freshly ground black pepper to taste |
| **To Garnish:** | **To Garnish:** |
| 4 tablespoons natural yogurt | ¹⁄₄ cup unflavored yogurt |
| 1 tablespoon snipped chives | 1 tablespoon snipped chives |

Wash and roughly chop the tomatoes and put them in a blender goblet with the yogurt. Blend very briefly and strain the mixture into a bowl. Add the remaining ingredients and mix well together. Chill thoroughly. Top each serving with a tablespoon of yogurt and sprinkle with snipped chives.

**Serves 4**

FROM REAR CLOCKWISE: AVOCADO GAZPACHO; ICED WALNUT SOUP *(page 34)*; VICHYSSOISE *(page 31)* AND CHILLED TOMATO SOUP

# Iced Walnut Soup

| METRIC/IMPERIAL | AMERICAN |
|---|---|
| 2 tablespoons olive oil | 2 tablespoons olive oil |
| 1 large onion, chopped | 1 large onion, chopped |
| 50 g/2 oz shelled walnuts | ½ cup shelled walnuts |
| 900 ml/1½ pints chicken stock | 3¾ cups chicken stock |
| 150 ml/¼ pint natural yogurt, beaten until liquid | ⅔ cup unflavored yogurt, beaten until liquid |
| 150 ml/¼ pint single cream | ⅔ cup light cream |
| salt to taste | salt to taste |
| freshly ground black pepper to taste | freshly ground black pepper to taste |

Heat the oil in a large pan, add the onion and cook gently until the onion is soft but not browned. Add the walnuts and sauté them with the onions for a minute or two, then add the stock. Bring the mixture to the boil, reduce the heat and simmer for 5 minutes. Cool.

Pour the mixture into a blender goblet and blend until smooth. Strain the mixture, then add the yogurt, cream, salt and pepper. Mix well together and pour into a serving dish. Chill well.
**Serves 4-6**

# A Taste of Turtle

| METRIC/IMPERIAL | AMERICAN |
|---|---|
| 150 ml/¼ pint water | ⅔ cup water |
| 1 tablespoon gelatine | 1 tablespoon unflavored gelatin |
| 1 × 400 g/14 oz can clear turtle soup | 1 × 14 oz can clear turtle soup |
| 100 g/4 oz yogurt curd cheese (see page 12) or cream cheese | ½ cup yogurt curd cheese (see page 12) or cream cheese |
| 150 ml/¼ pint natural yogurt | ⅔ cup unflavored yogurt |
| 1 teaspoon garlic salt | 1 teaspoon garlic salt |
| ¼ teaspoon curry powder | ¼ teaspoon curry powder |
| ½ teaspoon Tabasco sauce | ½ teaspoon Tabasco sauce |
| **To Garnish:** | **To Garnish:** |
| 1 × 100 g/4 oz jar lumpfish roe or thin slices of cucumber or lemon | 1 × ¼ lb jar lumpfish roe or thin slices of cucumber or lemon |

Put the water in a small saucepan and sprinkle the gelatine on it. When it has swollen, heat the mixture to dissolve the gelatine. Combine the gelatine and remaining ingredients and purée quickly in a blender or whisk until smooth.

Divide the consommé between 6 small ramekins or bowls and chill until set. Just before serving, top each serving with a spoonful of lumpfish roe or thin slices of cucumber or lemon.
**Serves 6**

# Chilled Cucumber and Mint Soup

METRIC/IMPERIAL
1 cucumber, peeled and diced
salt to taste
1-2 cloves garlic, peeled
900 ml/1 ½ pints natural yogurt
3 tablespoons finely chopped fresh
  mint
freshly ground black pepper to taste
6 sprigs of mint to garnish

AMERICAN
1 cucumber, peeled and diced
salt to taste
1-2 cloves garlic, peeled
3¾ cups unflavored yogurt
3 tablespoons finely chopped fresh
  mint
6 sprigs of mint to garnish

Sprinkle the cucumber with salt and leave it to drain for about 30 minutes.

Crush the garlic with a little salt. Combine the crushed garlic with the yogurt and mix well. Drain the cucumber and add it to the yogurt. Finally add the mint and salt and pepper to taste. Mix well and chill the mixture for an hour or more before serving. Top each portion with a sprig of fresh mint.
**Serves 6**

# Chicken and Lemon Soup

METRIC/IMPERIAL
600 ml/1 pint chicken stock
1 lemon
salt to taste
freshly ground black pepper to taste
50 g/2 oz long-grain rice
600 ml/1 pint natural yogurt
1 tablespoon cornflour
3 tablespoons water
2 egg yolks, beaten
2 tablespoons chopped parsley

AMERICAN
2½ cups chicken stock
1 lemon
salt to taste
freshly ground black pepper to taste
¼ cup long-grain rice
2½ cups unflavored yogurt
1 tablespoon cornstarch
3 tablespoons water
2 egg yolks, beaten
2 tablespoons chopped parsley

Put the stock in a large pan with the juice and finely grated rind of the lemon. Season to taste and bring to the boil. Wash the rice and add it to the boiling stock. Reduce the heat, cover and simmer until the rice is tender.

Tip the yogurt into a separate pan and whisk until it is liquid. Combine the cornflour (cornstarch) and water and mix with the yogurt. Beat in the egg yolks. Heat the mixture slowly to boiling, stirring in one direction only until it thickens.

Gradually add the yogurt mixture to the chicken soup, stirring constantly. Adjust the seasoning, and just before serving, stir in the parsley.
**Serves 4-6**

# Cream of Mushroom Soup

| METRIC/IMPERIAL | AMERICAN |
| --- | --- |
| 40 g/1½ oz butter | 3 tablespoons butter |
| 1 onion, finely chopped | 1 onion, finely chopped |
| 500 g/1 lb mushrooms, sliced | 1 lb mushrooms, sliced |
| 900 ml/1½ pints milk | 3¾ cups milk |
| 1 chicken stock cube | 1 chicken bouillon cube |
| salt to taste | salt to taste |
| freshly ground black pepper to taste | freshly ground black pepper to taste |
| 250 ml/8 fl oz stabilized yogurt | 1 cup stablilized yogurt |
| 2 tablespoons chopped parsley | 2 tablespoons chopped parsley |

Melt the butter in a large saucepan and add the onion. Sauté the onion gently until it is soft and slightly browned, then add the mushrooms. Cover, and cook on a low heat, shaking the pan from time to time, for about 10 minutes. Add the milk and stock (bouillon) cube, stir, bring to the boil, and reduce the heat. Season to taste with salt and pepper and simmer for another 5 minutes.

Just before serving, stir in the yogurt and parsley. Reheat and serve immediately.

**Serves 4-6**

# Prawn (Shrimp) Chowder

| METRIC/IMPERIAL | AMERICAN |
| --- | --- |
| 40 g/1½ oz butter | 3 tablespoons butter |
| 3 rashers streaky bacon, chopped | 3 slices fatty bacon, chopped |
| 500 g/1 lb potatoes, peeled and diced | 1 lb potatoes, peeled and diced |
| 1 large onion, chopped | 1 large onion, chopped |
| 900 ml/1½ pints milk | 3¾ cups milk |
| 1 bay leaf | 1 bay leaf |
| 225 g/8 oz cooked, peeled prawns | 1½ cups cooked, shelled shrimp |
| 250 ml/8 fl oz natural yogurt | 1 cup unflavored yogurt |
| salt to taste | salt to taste |
| freshly ground black pepper to taste | freshly ground black pepper to taste |
| 2 tablespoons snipped chives | 2 tablespoons snipped chives |

Melt the butter in a large pan and add the bacon, potatoes and onion. Sauté the mixture gently until the onions are soft but not browned. Add the milk and bay leaf, bring to the boil, cover and simmer for about 30 minutes or until the potatoes are tender.

Take out the bay leaf. Add the prawns (shrimp) and yogurt and season to taste with salt and pepper. Heat gently until the prawns (shrimp) are hot but do not allow to boil.

Serve immediately with a sprinkling of chopped parsley or chives.

**Serves 4-6**

FROM REAR: CHICKEN AND LEMON SOUP *(page 35)*; CREAM OF MUSHROOM SOUP AND PRAWN (SHRIMP) CHOWDER

# POULTRY AND MEAT

## Chicken in Tarragon Sauce

| METRIC/IMPERIAL | AMERICAN |
|---|---|
| *4 chicken escalopes* | *4 chicken scallops* |
| *50 g/2 oz butter* | *¼ cup butter* |
| *1 medium onion, finely chopped* | *1 medium onion, finely chopped* |
| *1 clove garlic, finely chopped* | *1 clove garlic, finely chopped* |
| *300 ml/½ pint chicken stock* | *1¼ cups chicken stock* |
| *1 tablespoon chopped fresh tarragon* | *1 tablespoon chopped fresh tarragon* |
| *  or 1 teaspoon dried* | *  or 1 teaspoon dried* |
| *300 ml/½ pint natural yogurt* | *1¼ cups unflavored yogurt* |
| *1 tablespoon cornflour* | *1 tablespoon cornstarch* |
| *2 egg yolks* | *2 egg yolks* |
| *salt to taste* | *salt to taste* |
| *freshly ground black pepper to taste* | *freshly ground black pepper to taste* |

Dry the chicken escalopes (scallops) with absorbent kitchen paper. Melt the butter in a frying pan (skillet) or sauté dish and when it froths well, add the chicken. Brown the escalopes (scallops) on both sides and transfer them to a warm dish. Keep warm.

Add the onion and garlic to the pan and fry gently on a low heat until the onion is soft but not browned. Add the chicken stock and tarragon and bring to the boil. Return the chicken pieces to the pan, lower the heat, and simmer gently until the chicken is cooked, about 10 minutes.

Transfer the chicken to a warm serving dish and keep warm. Combine the yogurt, cornflour (cornstarch) and egg yolks and beat lightly together. Gradually add the yogurt mixture to the liquid in the pan, stirring constantly. Cook gently until the mixture thickens. Season the sauce to taste with salt and pepper, then pour it over the chicken.

Serve chicken in tarragon sauce with plain boiled rice.
**Serves 4**

# Meatballs in Piquant Sauce

**METRIC/IMPERIAL**
1 large onion, finely minced
500 g/1 lb finely minced lean beef
  or lamb
100 g/4 oz fresh breadcrumbs
1 egg, beaten
2 tablespoons chopped parsley
1 tablespoon chopped fresh mint, or
  1 teaspoon dried
1 tablespoon chopped fresh oregano,
  or 1 teaspoon dried
salt to taste
freshly ground black pepper to taste
25 g/1 oz flour
4 tablespoons olive oil
150 ml/¼ pint natural yogurt
1 tablespoon cornflour
150 ml/¼ pint water
2 spring onions, finely chopped, to
  garnish

**AMERICAN**
1 large onion, finely ground
1 lb finely ground lean beef or lamb
2 cups fresh bread crumbs
1 egg, beaten
2 tablespoons chopped parsley
1 tablespoon chopped fresh mint, or
  1 teaspoon dried
1 tablespoon chopped fresh oregano,
  or 1 teaspoon dried
salt to taste
freshly ground black pepper to taste
¼ cup flour
¼ cup olive oil
⅔ cup unflavored yogurt
1 tablespoon cornstarch
⅔ cup water
2 scallions, finely chopped, to
  garnish

Combine the onion, meat, breadcrumbs, egg, parsley, mint, oregano, salt and pepper in a large bowl and mix well together. Form the mixture into balls, taking a large teaspoonful at a time and rolling it in the palms of your hands, then in flour.

Heat the oil in a sauté pan or heavy flameproof dish and fry the balls, a few at a time, for about 2 minutes on each side, then transfer the meatballs to a warm dish and keep warm.

Combine the yogurt, cornflour (cornstarch) and water and whisk lightly together. Add to the pan juices, and heat together, stirring, until the sauce thickens. Adjust the seasoning. Return the meatballs to the pan and stir gently to coat them with the sauce. Sprinkle the chopped spring onions (scallions) over the dish and serve immediately on buttered spaghetti or noodles.

**Serves 4**

# Tandoori Chicken

| METRIC/IMPERIAL | AMERICAN |
|---|---|
| 6 chicken legs | 6 chicken legs |
| 3 chicken breasts | 3 chicken breasts |
| **Marinade:** | **Marinade:** |
| 1 onion, peeled and coarsely chopped | 1 onion, peeled and coarsely chopped |
| 5 cloves garlic, peeled and coarsely chopped | 5 cloves garlic, peeled and coarsely chopped |
| 25 g/1 oz fresh green ginger, peeled and coarsely chopped | 2 tablespoons chopped fresh green ginger |
| 250 ml/8 fl oz natural yogurt | 1 cup unflavored yogurt |
| 4 tablespoons lemon juice | 1/4 cup lemon juice |
| 4 tablespoons vegetable oil | 1/4 cup vegetable oil |
| 1 tablespoon ground coriander | 1 tablespoon ground coriander |
| 1 tablespoon ground turmeric | 1 tablespoon ground turmeric |
| 1 teaspoon ground cumin | 1 teaspoon ground cumin |
| 1/2 teaspoon grated nutmeg | 1/2 teaspoon grated nutmeg |
| 1/2 teaspoon ground cinnamon | 1/2 teaspoon ground cinnamon |
| 1/2 teaspoon freshly ground pepper | 1/2 teaspoon freshly ground pepper |
| 1/4 teaspoon ground cloves | 1/4 teaspoon ground cloves |
| 1/4 teaspoon cayenne pepper | 1/4 teaspoon cayenne pepper |
| 2 teaspoons salt | 2 teaspoons salt |
| **To Garnish:** | **To Garnish:** |
| 6 large lettuce leaves, shredded | 6 large lettuce leaves, shredded |
| 1 onion, cut into thin rings | 1 onion, cut into thin rings |
| 1 lemon, cut in wedges | 1 lemon, cut in wedges |

Divide each chicken portion into 2 pieces and remove the skin. Using a sharp knife, make 3 diagonal slashes on each piece, cutting about half way through to the bone.

To make the marinade, blend the onions, garlic and ginger with the yogurt until smooth using an electric blender. Transfer the mixture to a large bowl and stir in all the remaining ingredients.

Add the chicken pieces to the marinade, a piece at a time, rubbing the mixture into the slashes. Cover the bowl and refrigerate for about 24 hours, turning the pieces 2 or 3 times.

To cook the chicken, lift the pieces from the marinade wiping off any excess and arrange them on the barbecue grid or grill (broiler) pan. Grill (broil) the chicken on a high heat for 5 minutes on each side to seal in the juices. Continue cooking on a lower heat until the meat is cooked through.

Arrange the shredded lettuce on a serving plate and top with the hot chicken. Garnish with onion rings and lemon wedges.

Serve tandoori chicken Indian fashion with fresh *naan* bread (see page 86) and cucumber *raita* (see page 74).
**Serves 6**

TANDOORI CHICKEN: TANDOORI PRAWNS (SHRIMP) *(page 58)*; NAAN *(page 86)* AND CUCUMBER RAITA *(page 74)*

# Beef Stroganoff

Make this quick recipe with tender steak, fillet, sirloin or rump. Beef Stroganoff is a very good way of stretching steak for unexpected guests.

| METRIC/IMPERIAL | AMERICAN |
|---|---|
| 500 g/1 lb steak | 1 lb steak |
| 50 g/2 oz butter | ¼ cup butter |
| 1 onion, finely chopped | 1 onion, finely chopped |
| 225 g/8 oz mushrooms, thinly sliced | ½ lb mushrooms, thinly sliced |
| 2 tablespoons brandy or dry sherry | 2 tablespoons brandy or dry sherry |
| 1 teaspoon English mustard | 1 teaspoon English mustard |
| 150 ml/¼ pint natural yogurt | ⅔ cup unflavored yogurt |
| 150 ml/¼ pint soured cream | ⅔ cup sour cream |
| 2 tablespoons cornflour | 2 tablespoons cornstarch |
| salt to taste | salt to taste |
| freshly ground black pepper to taste | freshly ground black pepper to taste |

Trim the steak and beat it flat between two sheets of greaseproof (wax) paper. Cut the meat into short, narrow strips and set it aside.

Melt 25 g/1 oz/2 tablespoons of the butter in a large sauté pan or frying pan (skillet), add the onion and fry gently until soft and just beginning to brown. Add the mushrooms and cook gently, turning the mixture from time to time until the mushrooms are soft. Using a slotted spoon transfer the vegetables to a dish and keep warm.

Add the remaining butter to the pan, raise the heat and add the steak. Brown it quickly on all sides, then reduce the heat and stir in the onion and mushroom mixture, the brandy or sherry, and the mustard.

Combine the yogurt, soured cream and cornflour (cornstarch) and add to the mixture in the pan. Season the sauce to taste with salt and pepper and stir over a low heat until the sauce is hot and slightly thickened.

Serve immediately with plain boiled rice, noodles or mashed potato.

**Serves 4-6**

# Kidneys in Mustard Sauce

The price of calf kidneys varies enormously with local demand. If they are too expensive, or not available, substitute 4 to 6 lambs' kidneys for each calf kidney.

| METRIC/IMPERIAL | AMERICAN |
| --- | --- |
| 3 calves' kidneys | 3 calves kidneys |
| 50 g/2 oz butter | ¼ cup butter |
| 2 large onions, finely chopped | 2 large onions, finely chopped |
| 300 ml/½ pint dry white wine | 1 ¼ cups dry white wine |
| 150 ml/¼ pint water | ⅔ cup water |
| 150 ml/¼ pint natural yogurt | ⅔ cup unflavored yogurt |
| 1 tablespoon cornflour | 1 tablespoon cornstarch |
| 1 tablespoon mustard powder | 1 tablespoon mustard powder |
| freshly ground black pepper to taste | freshly ground black pepper to taste |
| salt to taste | salt to taste |

Remove all fat and membranes from the kidneys and cut them into small pieces, set aside.

Melt the butter in a flameproof casserole and add the onions. Fry the onions over a low heat until they are soft but not browned. Raise the heat and add the kidneys. Fry them quickly, turning the pieces constantly for 2 minutes. Add the wine and water, and immediately the mixture comes to the boil, reduce the heat until the liquid barely simmers.

Combine the yogurt with the cornflour (cornstarch) and mustard. Stir gradually into the casserole and season the sauce to taste with pepper only. (Salt and too much heat both toughen the kidneys.)

Cover the casserole and put it in a preheated, very cool oven (120°C/250°F, Gas Mark ½) for 1 hour. Just before serving, season with salt and a little more freshly ground black pepper.

Serve with triangles of bread, fried in butter, and boiled rice.

**Serves 6**

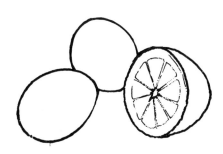

# Marinated Lamb Kebabs

The flavour of these kebabs is improved even more by cooking them over charcoal.

METRIC/IMPERIAL
4 tablespoons olive oil
150 ml/¼ pint natural yogurt
2 cloves garlic, crushed
2 tablespoons chopped parsley
freshly ground black pepper to taste
salt to taste
750 g/1½ lb boneless leg of lamb,
  cut into cubes
16 small mushrooms
2 medium onions, quartered
1 large green pepper, deseeded and
  cut in 8 strips
1 lemon, quartered, to garnish

AMERICAN
¼ cup olive oil
⅔ cup unflavored yogurt
2 cloves garlic, crushed
2 tablespoons chopped parsley
freshly ground black pepper to taste
salt to taste
1½ lb boneless leg of lamb, cut into
  cubes
16 small mushrooms
2 medium onions, quartered
1 large green pepper, deseeded and
  cut in 8 strips
1 lemon, quartered, to garnish

Combine the oil, yogurt, garlic, parsley, pepper and salt in a bowl and mix well. Add the lamb and mushrooms. Turn them in the marinade, cover the bowl and leave it in a cool place for at least 2 hours, or overnight. Stir the mixture once or twice as it marinates.

Blanch the onions and pieces of pepper by dropping them into boiling water for 2 minutes. Drain and reserve.

Thread the meat and vegetables on to skewers and grill (broil) on a high heat until the meat is well browned on the outside, juicy and pink in the middle.

Serve the kebabs with lemon wedges, hot Arab bread or *naan* (see page 86), or rice, and plenty of crisp green salad.
**Serves 4**

# Moussaka

Aubergine (eggplant) is an essential ingredient of a real Balkan *moussaka,* but if it is unobtainable, or too expensive, try using courgettes (zucchini) or slices of fried potato.

| METRIC/IMPERIAL | AMERICAN |
|---|---|
| *500 g/1 lb aubergines* | *1 lb eggplant* |
| *salt* | *salt* |
| *120 ml/4 fl oz olive oil* | *½ cup olive oil* |
| *500 g/1 lb onions, chopped* | *1 lb onions, chopped* |
| *500 g/1 lb cooked lamb, minced finely* | *2 cups finely ground cooked lamb* |
| *1 tablespoon chopped fresh marjoram, or 1 teaspoon dried* | *1 tablespoon chopped fresh marjoram, or 1 teaspoon dried* |
| *1 tablespoon chopped parsley* | *1 tablespoon chopped parsley* |
| *freshly ground black pepper to taste* | *freshly ground black pepper to taste* |
| *300 ml/½ pint chicken stock* | *1¼ cups chicken stock* |
| *600 ml/1 pint natural yogurt* | *2½ cups unflavored yogurt* |
| *2 egg yolks* | *2 egg yolks* |
| *1 tablespoon cornflour* | *1 tablespoon cornstarch* |
| *2 tablespoons water* | *2 tablespoons water* |
| *grated nutmeg to taste* | *grated nutmeg to taste* |

Wash the aubergines (eggplants), trim off the stalks, and slice them thinly. Lay the aubergine (eggplant) rounds in a colander, salting each layer, and set aside for 30 minutes for the salt to draw out some of the moisture.

Heat half the oil in a frying pan (skillet), rinse and dry the aubergine (eggplant) slices and fry them until golden, a few at a time, adding more oil as needed. Drain the fried aubergines (eggplants) on absorbent kitchen paper.

Fry the onions gently in the remaining oil until they are soft and slightly browned. Combine the onions, lamb, marjoram and parsley and season to taste with salt and pepper.

Grease an ovenproof dish about 7.5 cm/3 inches deep, and about 2.75 litre/5 pint/12 cups capacity. Lay half the aubergine (eggplant) slices in the bottom, and top with half the lamb, then the remaining aubergine (eggplant) slices, and finally the remaining lamb. Pour over the stock.

Put the yogurt in a bowl and whisk in the egg yolks. Mix the cornflour (cornstarch) with the water and whisk the mixture into the yogurt. Season lightly with salt and pepper.

Pour the yogurt topping in an even layer over the meat and sprinkle with a little grated nutmeg. Bake the moussaka in a preheated moderate oven (180°C/350°F, Gas Mark 4) for about 1 hour, until bubbling and golden. Serve with a green salad.
**Serves 4–6**

# Pork Chops en Papillote

| METRIC/IMPERIAL | AMERICAN |
|---|---|
| 4 large pork chops | 4 large pork chops |
| 25 g/1 oz butter | 2 tablespoons butter |
| 4 rectangles buttered foil, about | 4 rectangles buttered foil, about |
| 30 × 20 cm/12 × 8 inch | 12 × 8 inch |
| 1 large onion, chopped | 1 large onion, chopped |
| 250 g/8 oz mushrooms, sliced | ½ lb mushrooms, sliced |
| 150 ml/¼ pint natural yogurt | ⅔ cup unflavored yogurt |
| 150 ml/¼ pint single cream | ⅔ cup light cream |
| 50 g/2 oz fresh breadcrumbs | 1 cup fresh bread crumbs |
| 1 teaspoon made mustard | 1 teaspoon made mustard |
| salt to taste | salt to taste |
| freshly ground black pepper to taste | freshly ground black pepper to taste |
| grated nutmeg to taste | grated nutmeg to taste |

Trim any skin and excess fat from the chops and nick the fat edge at 1.5 cm/½ inch intervals. Melt the butter in a frying pan (skillet) and quickly brown the chops on each side. Using a fork or slotted spoon lift the chops from the pan and lay one chop on each piece of foil.

Add the onion to the butter remaining in the pan and sauté gently until it is soft but not brown. Add the mushrooms, cover, and shake the pan to distribute the remaining fat. Cook on a low heat until the mushroom juices run, about 5 minutes.

In a bowl combine the yogurt, cream and breadcrumbs. Stir this mixture gradually into the pan, still on a low heat. Stir in the mustard and season to taste with salt, freshly ground black pepper and a little grated nutmeg.

Divide the mixture between the 4 pork chops, slipping a spoonful under each chop and the remainder on top. Fold the foil twice at each edge to make secure parcels.

Arrange the parcels on a baking sheet and bake in a preheated cool oven (150°C/300°F, Gas Mark 2) for about 45 minutes.

Serve the chops in their foil parcels with baked, creamed or new potatoes and a green vegetable or salad.
**Serves 4**

# Spiced Roast Lamb

Spit-roasting is the ideal way of cooking a boned leg of lamb. But it may also be roasted on a rack in the oven with a tin underneath to catch the drippings.

| METRIC/IMPERIAL | AMERICAN |
|---|---|
| *1.5 kg/3 lb leg of lamb, boned* | *3 lb leg of lamb, boned* |
| *25 g/1 oz green ginger, peeled and finely grated* | *1 oz green ginger, peeled and finely grated* |
| *1 teaspoon salt* | *1 teaspoon salt* |
| *25 g/1 oz butter* | *2 tablespoons butter* |
| *2 medium onions, finely chopped* | *2 medium onions, finely chopped* |
| *2 tablespoons ground coriander* | *2 tablespoons ground coriander* |
| **To Baste:** | **To Baste:** |
| *150 ml/¼ pint natural yogurt* | *⅔ cup unflavored yogurt* |
| *100 g/4 oz butter, melted* | *½ cup melted butter* |
| *2 tablespoons ground cumin* | *2 tablespoons ground cumin* |
| *1 teaspoon ground cardamom* | *1 teaspoon ground cardamom* |
| *1 teaspoon ground cinnamon* | *1 teaspoon ground cinnamon* |
| *½ teaspoon ground cloves* | *½ teaspoon ground cloves* |

Trim the lamb, remove any skin, and lay it out flat, slashing the meat where necessary. Mix together the ginger and salt and rub this mixture into the meat on all sides. Set aside.

Melt the butter in a pan, add the onions, and fry gently until the onions are soft. Add the coriander and continue frying until the onions are well browned. Spread this mixture on one side of the meat, roll it up with the onion on the inside, and tie securely with string.

To make the basting mixture combine the yogurt, melted butter, cumin, cardamom, cinnamon and cloves and mix well.

To spit-roast the meat, cook on the maximum heat for about 15 minutes, or until well browned, and complete cooking according to the manufacturer's directions for roast lamb, basting frequently with the yogurt mixture.

To roast in the oven, set the meat on a rack with a tin on the shelf below, and roast in a preheated, very hot oven (230°C/450°F, Gas Mark 8) for 15 minutes, or until well browned. Lower the heat to moderate (180°C/350°F, Gas Mark 4) and continue roasting for about 1 hour 45 minutes. Baste frequently with the yogurt mixture.

When the meat is cooked, set it aside to rest while you make the spiced gravy. Skim any excess fat from the pan juices and add to them about 150 ml/¼ pint/⅔ cup water, and any remaining basting liquid. Bring the mixture to the boil, scraping up the pan juices to make a rich gravy. Reduce the mixture to a thick sauce by fast boiling. Season to taste and serve with the sliced meat.
**Serves 6-8**

# Pork Medallions with Apple Rings

This method applies to other light, quickly cooked meats such as veal, turkey or chicken.

| METRIC/IMPERIAL | AMERICAN |
| --- | --- |
| 750 g/1½ lb pork fillet | 1½ lb pork fillet |
| 2 crisp eating apples | 2 crisp dessert apples |
| 50 g/2 oz butter | ¼ cup butter |
| 2 tablespoons vegetable oil | 2 tablespoons vegetable oil |
| 2 tablespoons brandy | 2 tablespoons brandy |
| 150 ml/¼ pint natural yogurt | ⅔ cup unflavored yogurt |
| 4 tablespoons double cream | ¼ cup heavy cream |
| 1 tablespoon cornflour | 1 tablespoon cornstarch |
| salt to taste | salt to taste |
| freshly ground black pepper to taste | freshly ground black pepper to taste |

Cut the pork across the grain in 6 mm/¼ inch thick slices. Lay the meat between sheets of oiled greaseproof (wax) paper and beat it flat. Core the apples, but do not peel them, and cut into 6 mm/¼ inch thick slices.

Melt 25 g/1 oz/2 tablespoons of the butter in a heavy frying pan (skillet) and sauté the apple rings until they are golden on both sides. Transfer them to a warm dish and keep warm.

Add the remaining butter and the oil to the pan and quickly fry the pork medallions, a few at a time, over a high heat. As soon as they are cooked, arrange the meat on a hot serving dish and top with the reserved fried apple. Keep warm.

Pour off any excess fat in the pan and return it to a low heat. Add the brandy and stir well to incorporate the pan juices. Combine the yogurt, cream and cornflour (cornstarch) and mix well together. Gradually add this mixture to the pan juices, stirring constantly until the mixture thickens a little. Season to taste with salt and pepper and pour the sauce over the pork and apples.

Serve at once with boiled rice or creamed potatoes.

**Serves 4-6**

# FISH

## Baked Cod Cutlets

| METRIC/IMPERIAL | AMERICAN |
|---|---|
| 2 tablespoons olive oil | 2 tablespoons olive oil |
| 1 large onion, sliced | 1 large onion, sliced |
| 1 clove garlic, crushed | 1 clove garlic, crushed |
| 1 × 400 g/14 oz can tomatoes, drained | 1 × 14 oz can tomatoes, drained |
| ½ teaspoon Tabasco sauce | ½ teaspoon Tabasco sauce |
| 1 tablespoon chopped fresh oregano, or 1 teaspoon dried | 1 tablespoon chopped fresh oregano, or 1 teaspoon dried |
| salt to taste | salt to taste |
| freshly ground black pepper to taste | freshly ground black pepper to taste |
| 4 cod cutlets | 4 cod cutlets |
| 150 ml/¼ pint natural yogurt | ⅔ cup unflavored yogurt |
| 50 g/2 oz fresh breadcrumbs | 1 cup fresh bread crumbs |
| 2 tablespoons freshly grated Parmesan cheese | 2 tablespoons freshly grated Parmesan cheese |

Heat the oil in a pan and add the onion rings. Fry them gently until they are soft, but not browned. Add the garlic, tomatoes, Tabasco sauce and oregano. Season to taste with salt and pepper and cook together for about 5 minutes.

Spread half the mixture in the base of a shallow ovenproof dish that will just hold the cutlets in one layer, and lay the cutlets on the sauce. Pour the remaining sauce over the fish. Beat the yogurt to a liquid and pour it over the fish. Sprinkle the dish with breadcrumbs then Parmesan cheese.

Bake the fish in a preheated, moderately hot oven (190°C/375°F, Gas Mark 5) for 20 to 30 minutes, or until the fish is cooked and the top browned.

**Serves 4**

# Posh Fish Pie

METRIC/IMPERIAL
*50 g/2 oz butter*
*25 g/1 oz flour*
*300 ml/½ pint milk*
*150 ml/¼ pint natural yogurt*
*150 ml/¼ pint white wine or*
  *chicken stock*
*350 g/12 oz cooked white fish,*
  *flaked*
*100 g/4 oz cooked shelled prawns*
*100 g/4 oz cooked white crab meat*
*100 g/4 oz cooked scallops, diced*
*2 tablespoons chopped spring onions*
*salt to taste*
*freshly ground black pepper to taste*
*375 g/13 oz frozen puff pastry*
*1 egg, beaten*

AMERICAN
*¼ cup butter*
*¼ cup flour*
*1 ¼ cups milk*
*⅔ cup unflavored yogurt*
*⅔ cup white wine or chicken stock*
*¾ lb cooked white fish, flaked*
*¼ lb cooked shelled shrimp*
*¼ lb cooked white crab meat*
*¼ lb cooked scallops, diced*
*2 tablespoons chopped scallions*
*salt to taste*
*freshly ground black pepper to taste*
*¾ lb frozen puff pastry*
*1 egg, beaten*

Melt the butter in a saucepan and stir in the flour. Cook the *roux* for a minute or two without allowing it to colour. Gradually add the milk, stirring constantly, followed by the yogurt and white wine or stock. Cook the sauce on a low heat for about 2 minutes then add the flaked fish, prawns (shrimp), crab, scallops and spring onions (scallions). Season to taste with salt and pepper and pour it into a pie dish. Set aside to cool.

Thaw and roll the pastry. Cut a narrow strip long enough to edge the dish. Dampen the lip of the dish with water and lay down the pastry strip. Dampen the pastry strip with egg and cover the pie with pastry. Trim and knock up the edge. Make a generous slit in the lid to let out the steam and decorate the crust with the pastry trimmings. Brush the top (not the edges) with egg and bake in a preheated hot oven (220°C/425°F, Gas Mark 7) for about 35 minutes, or until golden.
**Serves 4-6**

# Crab Pancakes (Crêpes)

METRIC/IMPERIAL
3 tablespoons plain flour
1/4 teaspoon salt
1 large egg
120 ml/4 fl oz milk
120 ml/4 fl oz natural yogurt
1 tablespoon olive oil
1 tablespoon brandy (optional)
butter for frying
**Filling:**
1 small onion, chopped
1 bay leaf
1 blade of mace (optional)
250 ml/8 fl oz milk
25 g/1 oz butter
2 tablespoons flour
2 tablespoons dry sherry
1 teaspoon Worcestershire sauce
1 teaspoon mustard powder
120 ml/4 fl oz natural yogurt
4 tablespoons grated Parmesan
  cheese
salt and ground pepper to taste
225 g/8 oz cooked white crab meat

AMERICAN
3 tablespoons all-purpose flour
1/4 teaspoon salt
1 large egg
1/2 cup milk
1/2 cup unflavored yogurt
1 tablespoon olive oil
1 tablespoon brandy (optional)
butter for frying
**Filling:**
1 small onion, chopped
1 bay leaf
1 blade of mace (optional)
1 cup milk
2 tablespoons butter
2 tablespoons flour
2 tablespoons dry sherry
1 teaspoon Worcestershire sauce
1 teaspoon mustard powder
1/2 cup unflavored yogurt
1/4 cup grated Parmesan cheese
salt and ground pepper to taste
1/2 lb cooked white crab meat

Sift the flour and salt into a bowl and make a well in the middle.
Drop in the egg. Combine the milk, yogurt, oil and brandy and mix.
Add the liquid to the bowl and whisk thoroughly to make a smooth,
thin batter. Leave it to stand for at least an hour. Use the batter to
make 8 pancakes (crêpes) and stack them with squares of greaseproof
(wax) paper between each.

To make the filling, put the onion, bay leaf, mace and milk in a
small pan and heat to boiling point then infuse for 30 minutes.

Melt the butter in a saucepan and stir in the flour. Cook the *roux*
for a minute or two without allowing it to colour, then gradually
add the strained milk, stirring constantly. Stir in the sherry,
Worcestershire sauce, mustard and yogurt. Add half the Parmesan
cheese and season to taste with salt and freshly ground black pepper.

Put the crab meat in a bowl and pour in half the sauce. Mix well
and divide the mixture between the 8 pancakes (crêpes). Roll up the
filled pancakes (crêpes) and arrange them in one layer in a shallow,
buttered ovenproof dish. Pour over the remaining sauce and sprinkle
with the rest of the Parmesan cheese.

Bake in a preheated hot oven (220°C/425°F, Gas Mark 7) for 10 to
15 minutes or until the sauce is bubbling and the topping is golden.
**Serves 4**

# Scampi (Jumbo Shrimp) au Gratin

This recipe will serve 6 as a first course, 4 as a main dish.

METRIC/IMPERIAL
750 g/1½ lb potatoes, boiled and
  mashed
150 g/5 oz butter
salt to taste
freshly ground black pepper to taste
1 medium onion, chopped
1 bay leaf
1 blade mace (optional)
450 ml/¾ pint milk
25 g/1 oz flour
150 ml/¼ pint natural yogurt
2 tablespoons brandy
50 g/2 oz freshly grated Parmesan
  cheese
500 g/1 lb uncooked scampi, shelled
½ teaspoon paprika

AMERICAN
3 cups mashed potatoes
¾ cup butter
salt to taste
freshly ground black pepper to taste
1 medium onion, chopped
1 bay leaf
1 blade mace (optional)
2 cups milk
¼ cup flour
⅔ cup unflavored yogurt
2 tablespoons brandy
½ cup freshly grated Parmesan
  cheese
1 lb uncooked jumbo shrimp,
  shelled
½ teaspoon paprika

Combine the mashed potatoes with 100 g/4 oz/½ cup of the butter and beat until smooth. Season to taste with salt and pepper. Pipe the potatoes round the edge of a shallow flameproof dish about 5 cm/2 inches deep with a capacity of about 2 litres/3½ pints/9 cups. Keep the dish warm while you prepare the filling.

Put the onion, bay leaf, mace and milk in a small pan and bring to the boil. Remove from the heat and set aside to infuse for about 15 minutes. Strain and reserve the milk.

Heat the remaining butter in a large saucepan and stir in the flour. Cook the *roux* for a minute or 2 without allowing it to colour, then gradually stir in the strained milk. When the sauce is smooth and thick, beat in the yogurt, brandy, and half the grated Parmesan cheese. Season to taste with salt and freshly ground black pepper. Add the scampi (jumbo shrimp) and cook gently in the sauce until they are opaque and curl up. Be careful not to overcook them or they will become tough.

Remove the serving dish from the oven. Pour the scampi (jumbo shrimp) and sauce into the potato nest. Sprinkle with the remaining Parmesan cheese and the paprika. Brown the top under a hot grill (broiler) and serve immediately.
**Serves 4–6**

# Prawn (Shrimp) Biriani

## METRIC/IMPERIAL
50 g/2 oz butter or vegetable oil
2 large onions, chopped
2 cloves garlic, finely chopped
1-2 tablespoons curry paste
225 g/8 oz potatoes, diced
1 green pepper, chopped
450 ml/¾ pint chicken stock
150 ml/¼ pint natural yogurt
salt to taste
freshly ground black pepper to taste
**For the pilau:**
50 g/2 oz butter
1 tablespoon ground turmeric
1 teaspoon caraway seeds
2 cinnamon sticks, broken
6 cloves
6 cardamom pods
350 g/12 oz basmati rice
300 ml/½ pint water
1 teaspoon salt
225 g/8 oz cooked, peeled prawns
2 hard-boiled eggs, quartered
**To Garnish:**
1 large onion, sliced
25 g/1 oz butter
cooked prawns in the shell

## AMERICAN
¼ cup butter or vegetable oil
2 large onions, chopped
2 cloves garlic, finely chopped
1-2 tablespoons curry paste
½ lb potatoes, diced
1 green pepper, chopped
2 cups chicken stock
⅔ cup unflavored yogurt
salt to taste
freshly ground black pepper to taste
**For the pilau:**
¼ cup butter
1 tablespoon ground turmeric
1 teaspoon caraway seeds
2 cinnamon sticks, broken
6 cloves
6 cardamom pods
¾ lb basmati rice
1¼ cups water
1 teaspoon salt
½ lb cooked, shelled shrimp
2 hard-cooked eggs, quartered
**To Garnish:**
1 large onion, sliced
2 tablespoons butter
cooked prawns in the shell

Heat the oil or butter in a heavy pan and fry the onions and garlic until golden. Stir in the curry paste and fry for a minute more before adding the potatoes, green pepper, stock and yogurt. Bring to the boil, adjust the seasoning, and simmer, covered, for at least an hour.

For the pilau, choose a heavy, flameproof casserole with a well-fitting lid. Melt the butter over a medium heat and stir in the turmeric, caraway seeds, cinnamon, cloves and cardamom pods. Wash and drain the rice and add it to the pot. Turn the rice in the spiced butter and when each grain is coated add the water and salt. Bring to the boil, lower the heat, cover and simmer until all the water has been absorbed. The rice should be just tender with each grain separate. Add more water to the rice if necessary.

Reduce the heat to the lowest setting and add the prawns (shrimp), stirring them into the rice with a fork. Top with the egg quarters, cover and leave for about 5 minutes to heat through.

Fry the onion rings in butter until they are a deep golden colour. Top the pilau with the fried onion rings and prawns (shrimp).
**Serves 4-6**

# Tandoori Prawns (Shrimp)

METRIC/IMPERIAL
*750 g/1½ lb very large, raw
  prawns*
*1 recipe tandoori marinade (see
  page 40)*
**To Garnish:**
*6 large lettuce leaves, shredded*
*1 onion, cut in thin rings*
*1 lemon, cut in wedges*

AMERICAN
*1½ lb very large, raw shrimp*
*1 recipe tandoori marinade (see
  page 40)*
**To Garnish:**
*6 large lettuce leaves, shredded*
*1 onion, cut in thin rings*
*1 lemon, cut in wedges*

Shell the prawns (shrimp), leaving the tails on, and removing the heads if necessary. Remove the gut thread by splitting each prawn (shrimp) half way through its thickness and washing it out under cold water. Dry on absorbent kitchen paper.

Prepare the marinade and add the prawns (shrimp). Cover and marinate for 2 to 4 hours.

To cook the prawns (shrimp), lift them from the marinade shaking off any excess and arrange them on a barbecue grid or grill (broiler) pan. Grill (broil) on a high heat for about 5 minutes on each side.

Arrange the shredded lettuce on a serving plate and top with the hot prawns (shrimp). Garnish with onion rings and lemon wedges.
**Serves 4-6**

# VEGETABLES

## Baked Mushrooms

Large, open mushrooms weighing up to 100 g/4 oz/¼ lb each are ideal for this recipe. Otherwise, use any open mushrooms large enough to take a spoonful of stuffing.

| METRIC/IMPERIAL | AMERICAN |
|---|---|
| *6-24 mushrooms, depending on size* | *6-24 mushrooms, depending on size* |
| *1 clove garlic, crushed* | *1 clove garlic, crushed* |
| *salt to taste* | *salt to taste* |
| *150 ml/¼ pint natural yogurt* | *⅔ cup unflavored yogurt* |
| *175 g/6 oz fresh breadcrumbs* | *3 cups fresh bread crumbs* |
| *4 rashers streaky bacon* | *4 slices fatty bacon* |
| *2 tablespoons melted bacon fat or butter* | *2 tablespoons melted bacon fat or butter* |
| *1 tablespoon chopped parsley* | *1 tablespoon chopped parsley* |
| *freshly ground black pepper to taste* | *freshly ground black pepper to taste* |

Wipe the mushrooms and trim the stalks level with the caps.

Combine the garlic, salt and yogurt and blend in the breadcrumbs. Grill the bacon until it is crisp and crumble it into the stuffing. Add the bacon fat or butter, parsley and black pepper to taste.

Divide the stuffing between the mushrooms and arrange them on a greased baking dish. Bake in a moderately hot oven (200°C/400°F, Gas Mark 6) for 10 to 15 minutes, or until the mushrooms are tender. The exact time will depend on the size of the mushrooms.

Serve baked mushrooms as a vegetable with any roast meat, or as an hors d'oeuvre.

**Serves 6**

# Cheese and Onion Relish

| METRIC/IMPERIAL | AMERICAN |
|---|---|
| 120 ml/4 fl oz natural yogurt | ½ cup unflavored yogurt |
| 1 tablespoon finely chopped onion | 1 tablespoon finely chopped onion |
| 175 g/6 oz grated Cheddar cheese | 1½ cups grated Cheddar cheese |
| salt to taste | salt to taste |
| freshly ground black pepper to taste | freshly ground black pepper to taste |
| cayenne pepper to taste | cayenne pepper to taste |

Combine all the ingredients and beat them until smooth, by hand or in a blender. Serve with hot baked potatoes.
**Serves 4-6**

# Herb and Onion Relish

| METRIC/IMPERIAL | AMERICAN |
|---|---|
| 250 ml/8 fl oz natural yogurt | 1 cup unflavored yogurt |
| 6 spring onions, finely chopped | 6 scallions, finely chopped |
| 2 tablespoons finely chopped parsley | 2 tablespoons finely chopped parsley |
| salt to taste | salt to taste |
| freshly ground black pepper to taste | freshly ground black pepper to taste |

Combine all the ingredients and mix well together. Chill for about an hour to allow the flavour to develop.
   Serve with hot baked potatoes.
**Serves 4-6**

# Bacon Relish

| METRIC/IMPERIAL | AMERICAN |
|---|---|
| 4 rashers streaky bacon | 4 slices fatty bacon |
| 2 spring onions, finely chopped | 2 scallions, finely chopped |
| 150 ml/¼ pint natural yogurt | ⅔ cup unflavored yogurt |
| 50 g/2 oz grated Cheddar cheese | ½ cup grated Cheddar cheese |
| salt to taste | salt to taste |
| freshly ground black pepper to taste | freshly ground black pepper to taste |

Grill the bacon until it is very crisp. Crumble it, and set aside. Combine the chopped spring onions (scallions) with the yogurt, cheese, salt and pepper and blend until smooth. Stir in the crumbled bacon. Serve with hot baked potatoes.
**Serves 4-6**

FROM REAR: FISTUQIA *(page 62)* AND RELISHES: CHEESE AND ONION, HERB AND ONION, BACON

# Fistuqia

If the beans have particularly tough skins peel them after cooking.

METRIC/IMPERIAL
*500 g/1 lb broad beans*
*75 g/3 oz boiled rice*
*1 clove garlic, crushed*
*150 ml/¼ pint natural yogurt*
*1 egg, beaten*
*salt to taste*
*freshly ground black pepper to taste*

AMERICAN
*1 lb lima beans*
*½ cup boiled rice*
*1 clove garlic, crushed*
*⅔ cup unflavored yogurt*
*1 egg, beaten*
*salt to taste*
*freshly ground black pepper to taste*

Boil the beans in unsalted water for 15 to 20 minutes, or until tender. Drain the beans and return them to the pan. Add the rice and mix together.

Mix the garlic with the yogurt and add to the beans. Stir over a low heat, but do not boil. Add the egg, salt and pepper, and continue cooking gently until the sauce thickens a little.

Serve immediately, or cool and serve chilled.
**Serves 4**

# Spiced Spinach

The flavour of spiced spinach goes particularly well with lamb. To roast the cumin seeds heat them in a heavy pan until the aroma is released and they start to turn colour. Grind them in a pepper grinder.

METRIC/IMPERIAL
*1 kg/2 lb fresh spinach*
*salt to taste*
*300 ml/½ pint natural yogurt*
*2 teaspoons freshly roasted ground*
  *cumin seeds, or grated nutmeg to*
  *taste*
*freshly ground black pepper to taste*

AMERICAN
*2 lb fresh spinach*
*salt to taste*
*1¼ cups unflavored yogurt*
*2 teaspoons freshly roasted ground*
  *cumin seeds, or grated nutmeg to*
  *taste*
*freshly ground black pepper to taste*

Wash the spinach thoroughly and place it into a large saucepan. Cover and cook only until the spinach wilts. Do not overcook it for this dish.

Tip the spinach into a colander and drain it well pressing out all the excess moisture. Mince or chop the spinach very finely and combine it with all the remaining ingredients. Mix together.

Reheat the mixture gently, but do not boil it, and serve immediately. Or cool the spiced spinach and serve it chilled.
**Serves 4-6**

# Leeks in Yogurt Sauce

METRIC/IMPERIAL
*8-12 slender leeks*
*2 tablespoons lemon juice*
*1 tablespoon wine or cider vinegar*
*2 sprigs parsley*
*1 sprig lemon thyme*
*1 teaspoon salt*
*6 peppercorns, crushed*
**Sauce:**
*300 ml/½ pint natural yogurt*
*4 egg yolks, beaten*
*1 tablespoon lemon juice*
*1 teaspoon mild mustard*
*salt to taste*
*freshly ground black pepper to taste*

AMERICAN
*8-12 slender leeks*
*2 tablespoons lemon juice*
*1 tablespoon wine or cider vinegar*
*2 sprigs parsley*
*1 sprig lemon thyme*
*1 teaspoon salt*
*6 peppercorns, crushed*
**Sauce:**
*1¼ cups unflavored yogurt*
*4 egg yolks, beaten*
*1 tablespoon lemon juice*
*1 teaspoon mild mustard*
*salt to taste*
*freshly ground black pepper to taste*

Trim the leeks. Slit them down the length of the green part leaving the white intact, and wash them carefully.

Combine the lemon juice, vinegar, parsley, thyme, salt and pepper with 600 ml/1 pint/2½ cups water, bring to the boil and simmer for 10 minutes.

Put the leeks in a large shallow pan or flameproof dish and pour over the strained stock. Bring to the boil, cover and simmer for 10 to 15 minutes, or until the leeks are tender but not mushy. (If you are serving the leeks cold, leave them to cool in the stock.) Drain the leeks and arrange them on a warm, or cold, serving dish.

To make the sauce combine all the ingredients in a bowl or double boiler and cook, stirring, over just simmering water until the sauce thickens. This will take 10 to 15 minutes.

Pour the sauce over the leeks and serve hot, or chill well. Serve either as a vegetable or a first course.
**Serves 4-6**

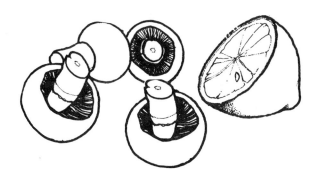

# Stuffed Courgettes (Zucchini)

Serve stuffed courgettes (zucchini), a Balkan and Middle Eastern dish, with boiled rice as a main course, or on their own as an hors d'oeuvre. The quantities given are for courgettes (zucchini) about 13 cm/5 inches long and 4 cm/1½ inches thick.

| METRIC/IMPERIAL | AMERICAN |
| --- | --- |
| 12 courgettes | 12 zucchini |
| salt to taste | salt to taste |
| 225 g/8 oz minced lean lamb or beef, cooked | ½ lb cooked ground lean lamb or beef |
| 100 g/4 oz rice, washed and cooked | 1 cup rice, washed and cooked |
| 2 tablespoons finely chopped parsley | 2 tablespoons finely chopped parsley |
| 2 tablespoons pine kernels (optional) | 2 tablespoons pine kernels (optional) |
| ½ teaspoon ground cinnamon | ½ teaspoon ground cinnamon |
| freshly ground black pepper to taste | freshly ground black pepper to taste |
| 300 ml/½ pint chicken or beef stock | 1½ cups chicken or beef stock |
| **Sauce:** | **Sauce:** |
| 600 ml/1 pint stabilized yogurt (see page 15) | 2½ cups stabilized yogurt (see page 15) |
| 2 cloves garlic | 2 cloves garlic |
| ½ teaspoon salt | ½ teaspoon salt |
| 25 g/1 oz butter | 2 tablespoons butter |
| 1 tablespoon chopped fresh mint or 1 teaspoon dried | 1 tablespoon chopped fresh mint or 1 teaspoon dried |

Trim the stems from the courgettes (zucchini). Cut off about 1.5 cm/½ inch from the stem ends and reserve these pieces as lids. Using an apple corer, or knife, scoop out the flesh from the middle of the vegetables and save it for another purpose. Salt the insides of the courgettes (zucchini) and set them aside to drain.

Combine the meat, rice, parsley, pine kernels, cinnamon and pepper in a bowl and mix very thoroughly together. Use this mixture to stuff the hollowed courgettes (zucchini).

Put the stuffed courgettes (zucchini) side by side in a casserole just large enough to hold them in 1 layer. Pour over the stock and bring to the boil. Cover and bake in a moderate oven (180°C/350°F, Gas Mark 4) for 1 hour.

Uncover the dish and pour the stabilized yogurt over the courgettes (zucchini). Cook, uncovered, for another 20 minutes.

Just before serving, crush the garlic with the salt. Heat the butter in a small pan and fry the garlic and mint together for 1–2 minutes. Pour over the courgettes (zucchini) and serve immediately.
**Serves 6**

STUFFED COURGETTES (ZUCCHINI) AND STUFFED PEPPERS
*(page 66)*

# Stuffed Peppers

METRIC/IMPERIAL
*4 green or red peppers, about*
  *100 g/4 oz each*
*3 tablespoons olive oil*
*1 large onion, chopped*
*75 g/3 oz fresh brown or white*
  *breadcrumbs*
*175 g/6 oz feta cheese, grated*
*100 g/4 oz yogurt curd cheese (see*
  *page 12)*
*1 tablespoon chopped parsley*
*1 tablespoon chopped fresh mint or*
  *1 teaspoon dried*
*1 tablespoon tomato purée*
*salt to taste*
*freshly ground black pepper to taste*

AMERICAN
*4 green or red peppers, about*
  *¼ lb each*
*3 tablespoons olive oil*
*1 large onion, chopped*
*1½ cups fresh brown or white bread*
  *crumbs*
*1½ cups grated feta cheese*
*½ cup yogurt curd cheese (see*
  *page 12)*
*1 tablespoon chopped parsley*
*1 tablespoon chopped fresh mint or*
  *1 teaspoon dried*
*1 tablespoon tomato paste*
*salt to taste*
*freshly ground black pepper to taste*

Cut the tops off the peppers at the stalk end to make lids, and pull out all the seeds and ribs. Blanch the peppers for 2 minutes in boiling water and drain upside down.

Heat 2 tablespoons of the oil and fry the onion until golden. Combine the fried onion with the breadcrumbs, feta, curd cheese, parsley, mint and tomato purée (paste). Season the stuffing to taste with salt and freshly ground black pepper.

Divide the stuffing between the peppers and replace the lids. Put the remaining oil in a casserole that will hold the peppers without too much room to spare and arrange the peppers upright in it. Cover and bake in a preheated moderate oven (180°C/350°F, Gas Mark 4) for 30 to 35 minutes, until tender.
**Serves 4**

# SALADS AND DRESSINGS

## Yogurt Mayonnaise

For a thick, glossy sauce to spoon on salmon and other dishes use thickened yogurt or, if you are using natural (unflavored) yogurt, add 1 teaspoon of unflavoured gelatine dissolved in 120 ml/4 fl oz/ ½ cup of water.

METRIC/IMPERIAL
*4 egg yolks*
*½ teaspoon powdered mustard*
*salt to taste*
*freshly ground black pepper to taste*
*1 teaspoon lemon juice*
*300 ml/½ pint olive oil*
*300 ml/½ pint natural yogurt, or*
  *freshly made thickened yogurt (see*
  *page 12)*

AMERICAN
*4 egg yolks*
*½ teaspoon powdered mustard*
*salt to taste*
*freshly ground black pepper to taste*
*1 teaspoon lemon juice*
*1¼ cups olive oil*
*1¼ cups unflavored yogurt, or*
  *freshly made thickened yogurt (see*
  *page 12)*

All the ingredients should be at room temperature before you begin.

Put the egg yolks in a medium bowl with the mustard and a pinch of salt and pepper. Work them to a smooth paste using a wire whisk or electric beater. Add the lemon juice and beat the mixture smooth again.

Now begin to add the olive oil, a drop at a time, beating in each addition vigorously. When about a quarter of the oil has been incorporated, add the remainder in a thin, steady stream. If the sauce becomes too thick before all the oil has been used, thin it down a little by beating in a very small quantity of the yogurt. Beat in the yogurt a tablespoon at a time.

Adjust the seasoning to taste. Cover the bowl to exclude the air, and chill the mixture thoroughly before serving. Tightly sealed, yogurt mayonnaise keeps for at least a week in the refrigerator.

# Hot Avocado Dressing

**METRIC/IMPERIAL**
*1 ripe avocado pear*
*1 tablespoon lemon juice*
*150 ml/¼ pint natural yogurt*
*Tabasco sauce to taste*
*salt to taste*

**AMERICAN**
*1 ripe avocado pear*
*1 tablespoon lemon juice*
*⅔ cup unflavored yogurt*
*Tabasco sauce to taste*
*salt to taste*

Scoop the flesh from the avocado and put it in a food processor or blender with all the other ingredients. Blend briefly. Check the seasoning and use immediately.
**Makes about 300 ml/½ pint/1¼ cups**

# Blue Cheese and Yogurt Dressing

**METRIC/IMPERIAL**
*1 tablespoon finely chopped onion*
*50 g/2 oz Roquefort or Danish blue*
  *cheese, crumbled*
*250 ml/8 fl oz natural yogurt*
*freshly ground black pepper to taste*

**AMERICAN**
*1 tablespoon finely chopped onion*
*½ cup crumbled Roquefort or*
  *Danish blue cheese*
*1 cup unflavored yogurt*
*freshly ground black pepper to taste*

Combine all the ingredients in a food processor or blender and mix until smooth. Alternatively, beat the dressing in a bowl until it is free of lumps. Chill thoroughly before serving.
**Makes about 300 ml/½ pint/1¼ cups**

# Fines Herbes Yogurt Dressing

**METRIC/IMPERIAL**
*150 ml/¼ pint natural yogurt*
*2 tablespoons chopped parsley*
*2 tablespoons chopped spring onions*
*2 tablespoons chopped dill*
*salt to taste*
*freshly ground black pepper to taste*

**AMERICAN**
*⅔ cup unflavored yogurt*
*2 tablespoons chopped parsley*
*2 tablespoons chopped scallions*
*2 tablespoons chopped dill*
*salt to taste*
*freshly ground black pepper to taste*

Combine all the ingredients and mix well together. Check the seasoning. Serve immediately, or store for up to a week in the refrigerator in a covered container.
**Makes about 150 ml/¼ pint/⅔ cup**

FROM REAR CLOCKWISE: HOT AVOCADO DRESSING; BLUE CHEESE AND YOGURT DRESSING; YOGURT MAYONNAISE *(page 67)* AND FINES HERBES YOGURT DRESSING

# Apple and Potato Salad

This salad is very good with cold roast chicken or with boiled ham.

METRIC/IMPERIAL
1 x 750 g/1½ lb can new potatoes
1 crisp eating apple, peeled
 and diced
2 tablespoons sultanas, plumped in
 boiling water
2 tablespoons coarsely chopped
 walnuts
150 ml/¼ pint yogurt mayonnaise
 (see page 67)
1 tablespoon sweet mango chutney
1 teaspoon curry paste
salt to taste
freshly ground black pepper to taste

AMERICAN
1 x 1½ lb can new potatoes
1 crisp dessert apple, peeled
 and diced
2 tablespoons seedless white raisins,
 plumped in boiling water
2 tablespoons coarsely chopped
 walnuts
⅔ cup yogurt mayonnaise (see
 page 67)
1 tablespoon sweet mango chutney
1 teaspoon curry paste
salt to taste
freshly ground black pepper to taste

Drain the potatoes. If they are very small leave whole, otherwise cut them in thick slices. Combine the potatoes, apple, plumped sultanas (seedless white raisins) and walnuts.

Mix together the yogurt mayonnaise, sweet mango chutney and curry paste. Add to the potato mixture and fold in thoroughly. Season to taste with salt and freshly ground black pepper. Chill before serving.
**Serves 4-6**

# Tuna Salad

METRIC/IMPERIAL
2 × 200 g/7 oz cans tuna
150 ml/¼ pint yogurt mayonnaise
 (see page 67)
2 tablespoons sweet lime pickle
1 gherkin, chopped
salt to taste
freshly ground black pepper to taste
½ cucumber, sliced, to garnish

AMERICAN
2 × 7 oz cans tuna
⅔ cup yogurt mayonnaise (see
 page 67)
2 tablespoons sweet lime pickle
1 dill pickle, chopped
salt to taste
freshly ground black pepper to taste
½ cucumber, sliced, to garnish

Drain the tuna and flake it into a bowl. Combine the yogurt mayonnaise with the sweet lime pickle, chopped gherkin (dill pickle), salt and pepper. Mix well and pour over the tuna. Fold together to coat the fish with dressing.

Arrange the sliced cucumber round a serving dish. Heap the tuna salad in the centre. Chill well.
**Serves 4**

# Summer Slaw

METRIC/IMPERIAL
500 g/1 lb hard white, cabbage,
  shredded
2 young carrots, grated
2 crisp eating apples, grated
3 tablespoons currants
3 tablespoons coarsely chopped
  walnuts
150 ml/¼ pint yogurt mayonnaise
  (see page 67)
salt to taste
freshly ground black pepper to taste

AMERICAN
1 lb hard white cabbage, shredded
2 young carrots, grated
2 crisp dessert apples, grated
3 tablespoons currants
3 tablespoons coarsely chopped
  walnuts
⅔ cup yogurt mayonnaise (see
  page 67)
salt to taste
freshly ground black pepper to taste

Combine all the ingredients in a large bowl and mix thoroughly.
Chill for 1-2 hours before serving to allow the flavours to mingle.
**Serves 4-6**

# Potato Salad

New or main crop potatoes can be used for potato salad. For the best
flavour, they should be mixed with the oil and vinegar dressing
while still warm.

METRIC/IMPERIAL
1 kg/2 lb boiled potatoes, whole or
  cut up
1 small onion, finely chopped
2 tablespoons olive oil
1 tablespoon wine vinegar
½ teaspoon salt
¼ teaspoon dry mustard
freshly ground black pepper to taste
150 ml/¼ pint yogurt mayonnaise
  (see page 67)
1 tablespoon chopped fresh chives or
  parsley to garnish

AMERICAN
2 lb boiled potatoes, whole or
  cut up
1 small onion, finely chopped
2 tablespoons olive oil
1 tablespoon wine vinegar
½ teaspoon salt
¼ teaspoon dry mustard
freshly ground black pepper to taste
⅔ cup yogurt mayonnaise (see
  page 67)
1 tablespoon chopped fresh chives or
  parsley to garnish

Combine the warm potatoes and onion in a bowl and mix.
  Shake together in a small jar the oil, vinegar, salt, mustard and
pepper, then pour this dressing over the potatoes. Turn the potatoes
in the dressing and set aside until quite cold.
  Fold in the yogurt mayonnaise. Turn the salad into a serving dish
and top with chopped chives or parsley. Serve potato salad at room
temperature.
**Serves 6-8**

# Mixed Bean Salad

All sorts of cooked beans make delicious salads, especially in winter when green salad stuffs are expensive and often disappointing. Canned beans should be well rinsed in cold water before using. Dried beans are best soaked overnight before boiling in unsalted water until tender.

| METRIC/IMPERIAL | AMERICAN |
| --- | --- |
| 225 g/8 oz cooked red kidney beans | ½ lb cooked red kidney beans |
| 225 g/8 oz cooked white haricot or cannellini beans | ½ lb cooked white navy or cannellini beans |
| 225 g/8 oz cooked green flageolet beans | ½ lb cooked green flageolet beans |
| 1 small onion, finely chopped | 1 small onion, finely chopped |
| 2 tablespoons chopped parsley | 2 tablespoons chopped parsley |
| 250 ml/8 fl oz yogurt mayonnaise (see page 67) | 1 cup yogurt mayonnaise (see page 67) |
| salt to taste | salt to taste |
| freshly ground black pepper to taste | freshly ground black pepper to taste |

Combine all the ingredients in a large bowl and mix well together. Serve at room temperature.
**Serves 6-8**

# Winter Slaw

Dressing for coleslaw does not have to be mayonnaise. Half in half yogurt mayonnaise and soured (sour) cream is one variation, a mixture of yogurt curd cheese and soured (sour) cream is another.

| METRIC/IMPERIAL | AMERICAN |
| --- | --- |
| 500 g/1 lb hard red or white cabbage, shredded | 1 lb hard red or white cabbage, shredded |
| 2 carrots, grated | 2 carrots, grated |
| 1 medium onion, grated | 1 medium onion, grated |
| 100 g/4 oz raw beetroot, grated | ¼ lb raw beet, grated |
| 100 g/4 oz raw parsnip, grated | ¼ lb raw parsnip, grated |
| 150 ml/¼ pint yogurt mayonnaise (see page 67) | ⅔ cup yogurt mayonnaise (see page 67) |
| salt to taste | salt to taste |
| freshly ground black pepper to taste | freshly ground black pepper to taste |

Combine all the ingredients in a large bowl and mix thoroughly. Chill for 1-2 hours before serving to allow the flavours to mingle.
**Serves 4-6**

FROM FRONT LEFT CLOCKWISE: POTATO SALAD AND SUMMER SLAW *(both page 71)*; MIXED BEAN SALAD AND WINTER SLAW

# Baltic Herring Salad

METRIC/IMPERIAL
1 crisp eating apple
1 crisp lettuce, coarsely shredded
1 large onion, thinly sliced
225 g/8 oz pickled herrings, sliced
4 tablespoons natural yogurt
4 tablespoons soured cream
freshly ground black pepper to taste
1 tablespoon chopped fresh dill or
  parsley to garnish

AMERICAN
1 crisp dessert apple
1 head crisp lettuce, coarsely
  shredded
1 large onion, thinly sliced
½ lb pickled herrings, sliced
¼ cup unflavored yogurt
¼ cup sour cream
freshly ground black pepper to taste
1 tablespoon chopped fresh dill or
  parsley to garnish

Peel and slice the apple and put the slices immediately into water acidulated with 1 tablespoon of lemon juice or vinegar.

Line a salad bowl with lettuce. Combine the onion rings, apples slices and herrings and arrange them in the centre of the bowl.

Combine the yogurt and soured (sour) cream. Add the pepper and beat lightly together. Pour the dressing over the herring mixture. Sprinkle the top with dill or parsley and chill well.

Serve herring salad with hot new potatoes tossed in butter or soured (sour) cream.
**Serves 2-4**

# Cucumber Raita

METRIC/IMPERIAL
1 cucumber, peeled, seeded
  and diced
salt
6 spring onions, chopped
2 tablespoons chopped fresh mint
250 ml/8 fl oz natural yogurt
freshly ground black pepper to taste
fresh mint or spring onion,
  chopped, to garnish

AMERICAN
1 cucumber, peeled, seeded
  and diced
salt
6 scallions, chopped
2 tablespoons chopped fresh mint
1 cup unflavored yogurt
freshly ground black pepper to taste
fresh mint or scallion, chopped, to
  garnish

Salt the diced cucumber and set it aside for about 30 minutes to allow the salt to draw the juices. Rinse and drain.

Combine the cucumber with the spring onions (scallions), mint and yogurt, and mix well. Season to taste with freshly ground black pepper, cover and chill.

Just before serving, top with fresh mint sprigs or chopped spring onion (scallion).
**Serves 4-6**

# North Sea Cod Salad

METRIC/IMPERIAL
750 g/1 ½ lb fresh cod
salt to taste
freshly ground black pepper to taste
250 ml/8 fl oz yogurt mayonnaise
  (see page 67)
2 tablespoons chopped spring onions
2 tablespoons capers
2 tablespoons chopped parsley
**To Garnish:**
1 head lettuce or chicory
sprigs of parsley

AMERICAN
1 ½ lb fresh cod
salt to taste
freshly ground black pepper to taste
1 cup yogurt mayonnaise (see
  page 67)
2 tablespoons chopped scallions
2 tablespoons capers
2 tablespoons chopped parsley
**To Garnish:**
1 head lettuce or Belgian endive
sprigs of parsley

Poach the fish in water to cover, lightly seasoned with salt and
pepper. Allow it to cool in the liquid, then remove all skin and bones
and flake the fish into a bowl.

Add the yogurt mayonnaise, spring onions (scallions), capers and
parsley and mix well. Adjust the seasoning to taste.

Line a serving bowl with lettuce or chicory (Belgian endive) and
heap the cod in the centre. Top with parsley sprigs. Chill. Serve as a
main course or hors d'oeuvre.
**Serves 4-6**

# Honey and Yogurt Salad Dressing

This is a lovely dressing for salads of fresh fruit and cottage cheese
served on a bed of crisp lettuce.

METRIC/IMPERIAL
150 ml/¼ pint natural yogurt
2 tablespoons runny honey
½ teaspoon ground cinnamon
1 teaspoon finely grated orange zest

AMERICAN
⅔ cup unflavored yogurt
2 tablespoons runny honey
½ teaspoon ground cinnamon
1 teaspoon finely grated orange zest

Combine all the ingredients in a small bowl and mix thoroughly.
Serve immediately or cover tightly and store in the refrigerator for
up to a week.
**Makes about 175 ml/6 fl oz/¾ cup**

# DESSERTS

## Light Lemon Cheesecake

**METRIC/IMPERIAL**
50 g/2 oz unsalted butter
150 g/6 oz shortcake biscuits,
  crushed
1 sachet gelatine
120 ml/4 fl oz water
2 eggs, separated
100 g/4 oz caster sugar
225 g/8 oz yogurt curd cheese (see
  page 12)
1 large lemon
300 ml/½ pint double cream
**To decorate:**
4 tablespoons shortcake biscuit
  crumbs
grapes, seeded and halved

**AMERICAN**
¼ cup sweet butter
6 oz shortcake cookies, crushed
1 sachet unflavored gelatin
½ cup water
2 eggs, separated
½ cup superfine sugar
½ lb yogurt curd cheese (see
  page 12)
1 large lemon
1¼ cups heavy cream
**To decorate:**
4 tablespoons shortcake cookie
  crumbs
grapes, seeded and halved

Melt the butter and stir in the crumbs. Mix well with a fork. Press the mixture over the bottom of a 20 cm/8 inch loose–bottomed cake tin (springform pan). Chill well.

Sprinkle the gelatine on to the water in a small pan and leave until swollen.

In a large bowl beat together the egg yolks and sugar until the mixture is pale and light. Heat the gelatine until the granules dissolve completely then whisk it into the egg mixture. Beat in the yogurt curd cheese and the juice and finely grated rind of the lemon.

Whip the cream until it holds a soft peak, and in another bowl, whisk the egg whites until stiff. Fold the cream and egg whites into the cheese mixture and whisk lightly together.

Pour the filling into the prepared tin, level the top and chill until set.

Just before serving, remove from the tin, press crumbs on to the sides and decorate the top of the cheesecake with grape halves.
**Serves 6-8**

PAVLOVA AND YOGURT CHANTILLY *(page 78)*;
LIGHT LEMON CHEESECAKE AND APRICOT MOUSSE *(page 82)*.

# Pavlova and Yogurt Chantilly

METRIC/IMPERIAL
**Meringue:**
*2 egg whites*
*1 teaspoon white wine vinegar*
*3 tablespoons hot water*
*350 g/12 oz caster sugar*
*1 teaspoon cornflour*
*½ teaspoon vanilla essence*
**For the yogurt chantilly:**
*150 ml/¼ pint double cream*
*150 ml/¼ pint natural yogurt*
*2 tablespoons sifted icing sugar*
*½ teaspoon vanilla essence*
**To decorate:**
*2 kiwi fruit, peeled and sliced*

AMERICAN
**Meringue:**
*2 egg whites*
*1 teaspoon white wine vinegar*
*3 tablespoons hot water*
*1½ cups superfine sugar*
*1 teaspoon cornstarch*
*½ teaspoon vanilla extract*
**For the yogurt chantilly:**
*⅔ cup heavy cream*
*⅔ cup unflavored yogurt*
*2 tablespoons sifted confectioners' sugar*
*½ teaspoon vanilla extract*
**To decorate:**
*2 kiwi fruit, peeled and sliced*

Combine all the meringue ingredients in a large bowl and beat them together until the mixture holds a firm peak (about 3 minutes with an electric beater).

Mark a circle about 20 cm/8 inch in diameter on a piece of kitchen foil and anchor it to a baking sheet with dabs of fat. Heap the meringue on to the foil and spread it as evenly as possible within the circle. Bake in a preheated very cool oven (120°C/250°F, Gas Mark ½) for 1½ hours. When cool transfer to a flat serving plate.

To make the topping, whip the cream until it holds a stiff peak. Fold in all the remaining ingredients and chill well.

Just before serving, pile the Yogurt Chantilly on to the Pavlova and arrange the sliced kiwi fruit over the top.
**Serves 4-6**

# Gooseberry Fool

METRIC/IMPERIAL
*500 g/1 lb gooseberries*
*100 g/4 oz sugar*
*4 tablespoons water*
*150 ml/¼ pint natural yogurt*
*150 ml/¼ pint double cream*

AMERICAN
*1 lb gooseberries*
*½ cup sugar*
*¼ cup water*
*⅔ cup unflavored yogurt*
*⅔ cup heavy cream*

Top and tail the gooseberries and put them in a saucepan with the sugar and water. Cover and cook gently until the fruit is pulpy. Sieve the purée and set it aside to cool.

Combine the cold gooseberry purée with the yogurt and mix well.

Whip the cream until it holds a stiff peak and fold it into the fruit mixture. Chill well before serving in individual bowls or glasses.
**Serves 6**

# Spiced Fruit Salad

| METRIC/IMPERIAL | AMERICAN |
|---|---|
| 600 ml/1 pint natural yogurt | 2½ cups unflavored yogurt |
| 4 tablespoons sugar | ¼ cup sugar |
| 1 teaspoon ground cinnamon | 1 teaspoon ground cinnamon |
| ½ teaspoon ground cardamom | ½ teaspoon ground cardamom |
| 2 ripe peaches or mangoes | 2 ripe peaches or mangoes |
| 2 seedless mandarin oranges | 2 seedless mandarin oranges |
| 225 g/8 oz seedless grapes | ½ lb seedless grapes |
| 225 g/8 oz strawberries or stoned cherries | ½ lb strawberries or pitted cherries |
| 1 crisp apple | 1 crisp apple |

Combine the yogurt, sugar, cinnamon and cardamom in a large bowl and mix well.

Peel, stone (pit) and chop the peaches or mangoes. Peel and chop the mandarin oranges, removing any pith or stringy bits. Wash the grapes and strawberries or cherries. Peel, core and chop the apple.

Add all the fruit to the yogurt mixture and mix. Chill for at least an hour before serving.

**Serves 6-8**

# Strawberry Yogurt Ice Cream

| METRIC/IMPERIAL | AMERICAN |
|---|---|
| 225 g/8 oz strawberries | 1½ cups strawberries |
| 100 g/4 oz sugar | ½ cup sugar |
| 300 ml/½ pint thickened yogurt (see page 12) or natural yogurt | 1¼ cups thickened yogurt (see page 12) or unflavored yogurt |
| 150 ml/¼ pint soured cream | ⅔ cup sour cream |
| 2 egg whites | 2 egg whites |
| 2 tablespoons icing sugar | 2 tablespoons confectioners' sugar |

Rub the strawberries through a sieve (strainer), or process them lightly in a blender and sieve (strain) the purée. Add the sugar, yogurt and soured (sour) cream and mix thoroughly. Refrigerate the mixture for about 30 minutes.

Whisk the egg whites until foamy, add the icing sugar and continue whisking until the meringue holds a stiff peak.

Combine the chilled strawberry yogurt with the meringue and beat lightly together.

Freeze in an electric ice cream maker. Or, alternatively, still-freeze whisking the mixture once or twice as it firms.

**Makes about 1 litre/1¾ pints/4¼ cups**

# Yogurt Brûlée

METRIC/IMPERIAL
*600 ml/1 pint milk*
*150 ml/¼ pint single cream*
*4 tablespoons powdered skimmed*
  *milk*
*1 tablespoon natural yogurt or*
  *powdered starter as directed*
*4-6 tablespoons caster sugar, for*
  *topping*

AMERICAN
*2½ cups milk*
*⅔ cup light cream*
*¼ cup powdered skimmed milk*
*1 tablespoon unflavored yogurt or*
  *powdered starter as directed*
*4-6 tablespoons sugar, for topping*

Combine the milk and cream in a saucepan and heat until almost
boiling. Remove from the heat immediately and set aside until it has
cooled to 40–43°C/105–110°F. (Use a thermometer for accuracy.) Stir
in the powdered skimmed milk and yogurt or powdered starter and
whisk lightly together.
   Pour the mixture into 6 ramekins, cover and incubate at
40–43°C/105–110°F for 6 to 10 hours or until firm. Chill very
thoroughly.
   About 2 hours before serving, preheat the grill (broiler) and
sprinkle 1 tablespoon of sugar on each ramekin. Arrange the dishes
in the grill (broiler) pan and grill (broil) the sugar as fast as possible
until it caramelizes and turns a rich golden brown. Return the
ramekins to the refrigerator immediately and chill well before
serving.
**Serves 6**

# Coeur á la Crème

METRIC/IMPERIAL
*225 g/8 oz yogurt curd cheese (see*
  *page 12)*
*300 ml/½ pint double cream*
*2 tablespoons caster sugar*

AMERICAN
*½ lb yogurt curd cheese (see*
  *page 12)*
*1¼ cups heavy cream*
*2 tablespoons superfine sugar*

Beat the yogurt curd cheese until smooth. Whip the cream until it
holds a soft peak. Combine the curd cheese, whipped cream and
sugar and beat lightly together.
   Line 6 *coeur à la crème* moulds or a sieve (strainer) with muslin
(cheesecloth) and spoon in the cream mixture. Press it into the
moulds and place the moulds in a container to catch the liquid.
Refrigerate for about 12 hours during which the mixture will firm up
and a little of its liquid will drain away.
   Turn out the moulds and serve chilled with strawberries and
sugar, or with cream and sugar.
**Serves 6**

# Apricot Mousse

METRIC/IMPERIAL
*1 sachet gelatine*
*120 ml/4 fl oz water*
*250 ml/8 fl oz sweetened apricot*
 *purée*
*2 eggs, separated*
*150 ml/¼ pint natural yogurt*
**Sauce:**
*120 ml/4 fl oz apricot jam*
*juice of 1 orange*

AMERICAN
*1 sachet unflavored gelatin*
*½ cup water*
*1 cup sweetened apricot purée*
*2 eggs, separated*
*⅔ cup unflavored yogurt*
**Sauce:**
*½ cup apricot jam*
*juice of 1 orange*

Sprinkle the gelatine on the water in a small saucepan and leave until swollen. Heat until the gelatine dissolves completely, then remove from the heat and set aside to cool.

Combine the apricot purée with the egg yolks, yogurt and dissolved gelatine and mix well.

Whisk the egg whites until they form stiff peaks and fold lightly into the apricot mixture. Pour the mousse into a wetted jelly mould or bowl of about 750 ml/1¼ pints/3 cups capacity and chill until set.

Turn out the mousse on to a serving plate. Just before serving, heat together the jam and orange juice. Strain and pour over the mousse.
**Serves 4-6**

# Cream Cheese Pancakes (Crêpes)

METRIC/IMPERIAL
*8 pancakes (see page 54)*
*100 g/4 oz yogurt curd cheese (see*
 *page 12)*
*150 ml/¼ pint double cream,*
 *whipped*
*2 tablespoons sugar*
*1 tablespoon finely grated lemon*
 *rind*
*2 tablespoons icing sugar*

AMERICAN
*8 crêpes (see page 54)*
*¼ lb yogurt curd cheese (see*
 *page 12)*
*⅔ cup heavy cream, whipped*
*2 tablespoons sugar*
*1 tablespoon finely grated lemon*
 *rind*
*2 tablespoons confectioners' sugar*

Make the pancakes (crêpes) as described on page 54 and keep them warm.

Combine the yogurt curd cheese with the whipped cream, sugar and lemon rind and beat lightly together.

Divide the cheese mixture between the pancakes, roll them up and dust them with icing (confectioners') sugar. Serve immediately.
**Serves 4**

# BAKING WITH YOGURT

# Rich Shortcrust Pastry (Enriched Basic Pie Dough)

Use this crisp shortcrust (basic pie dough) recipe for the sweet and savoury quiches and pies which follow. If using for savoury recipes, omit the sugar. Chilling the pastry for another 10 minutes after shaping and before baking helps to stop it shrinking.

| METRIC/IMPERIAL | AMERICAN |
|---|---|
| 225 g/8 oz plain flour | 2 cups all-purpose flour |
| 1 teaspoon icing sugar | 1 teaspoon confectioners' sugar |
| ½ teaspoon salt | ½ teaspoon salt |
| 100 g/4 oz chilled butter | ½ cup chilled butter |
| 1 egg yolk | 1 egg yolk |
| 2-3 tablespoons natural yogurt | 2-3 tablespoons unflavored yogurt |

Sift the flour, sugar and salt into a large bowl. Cut the butter in small dice and toss the pieces lightly in the flour. Rub in the fat, using a pastry blender or your finger tips, until the mixture resembles fine breadcrumbs.

Beat the egg yolk with 2 tablespoons of the yogurt and sprinkle over the flour mixture. Mix lightly together, adding a little more yogurt or water if needed.

Press the dough lightly into a ball and refrigerate it for 30 minutes wrapped in greaseprooof (wax) paper and a slightly damp tea-towel.

Knead the pastry very lightly just before rolling it out on a floured surface.

Use as directed.

**Makes 225 g/8 oz/½ lb pastry (dough)**

# Herb Quiche

If you are baking the quiche in a china dish rather than a tin increase the baking times of the unfilled pastry shell by 5 minutes at each stage.

| METRIC/IMPERIAL | AMERICAN |
|---|---|
| *1 recipe rich shortcrust pastry (see page 83)* | *1 recipe enriched basic pie dough (see page 83)* |
| *1 tablespoon butter* | *1 tablespoon butter* |
| *1 onion, finely chopped* | *1 onion, finely chopped* |
| *4 large eggs* | *4 large eggs* |
| *300 ml/½ pint milk* | *1¼ cups milk* |
| *150 ml/¼ pint natural yogurt* | *⅔ cup unflavored yogurt* |
| *150 ml/¼ pint double cream* | *⅔ cup heavy cream* |
| *50 g/2 oz freshly grated Parmesan or Gruyère cheese* | *½ cup freshly grated Parmesan or Gruyère cheese* |
| *4 tablespoons finely chopped fresh herbs: parsley, chives, thyme, chervil, tarragon etc.* | *¼ cup finely chopped fresh herbs: parsley, chives, thyme, chervil, tarragon, etc.* |
| *salt to taste* | *salt to taste* |
| *freshly ground black pepper to taste* | *freshly ground black pepper to taste* |

Lightly grease a 25 cm/10 inch flan ring (pie pan). Roll out the pastry thinly and rest it for 5 minutes before lifting it on the rolling pin and laying on the tin. Ease the pastry gently into shape without stretching it, trim the edges, and chill for another 10 minutes.

Just before baking the pastry shell, line it with greaseproof (wax) paper or foil and weight it with rice or baking beans. Bake, on a baking sheet, in a preheated, moderately hot oven (200°C/400°F, Gas Mark 6) for 10 minutes. Take it from the oven and remove the weights and lining paper. Lower the oven heat to moderate (180°C/350°F, Gas Mark 4) and bake for another 5 to 10 minutes.

While the pastry (dough) shell is baking, prepare the filling. Melt the butter in a small saucepan and fry the onion until soft without allowing it to brown.

Combine the eggs, milk, yogurt and cream and whisk lightly together. Add the onion, cheese and herbs and mix well. Season to taste with salt and freshly ground black pepper.

Take the pastry shell from the oven and pour in the filling. Return the quiche to the oven and bake for about 40 minutes, or until the filling is set.

Serve hot or cold with a crisp green salad or coleslaw.
**Serves 4-6**

# Naan

This yeast-raised bread is traditionally baked in a clay *tandoor* oven. Flat, tear-drop shaped pieces of dough are slapped on to the sides of the oven where they puff up and bake very fast. Grilling (broiling) is a successful alternative to *tandoor* baking. Serve *naan* piping hot.

| METRIC/IMPERIAL | AMERICAN |
|---|---|
| 175 ml/6 fl oz milk | 3/4 cup milk |
| 1 tablespoon sugar | 1 tablespoon sugar |
| 1 1/2 teaspoons dried yeast | 1 1/2 teaspoons active dry yeast |
| 1 egg, beaten | 1 egg, beaten |
| 2 tablespoons vegetable oil | 2 tablespoons vegetable oil |
| 4 tablespoons natural yogurt | 1/4 cup unflavored yogurt |
| 500 g/1 lb plain flour | 4 cups all-purpose flour |
| 1 teaspoon baking powder | 1 teaspoon baking powder |
| 1/2 teaspoon salt | 1/2 teaspoon salt |
| 1 tablespoon black onion seeds or 2 tablespoons chopped cashew nuts | 1 tablespoon black onion seeds or 2 tablespoons chopped cashew nuts |

Heat the milk to lukewarm, about 43°C/110°F and put it in a bowl with the sugar and yeast. Whisk the mixture and set it aside in a warm place for about 10 minutes, or until the yeast has dissolved and frothed up.

Stir in the egg, oil and the yogurt. Mix until well blended.

Sift together into a large bowl the flour, baking powder and salt. Make a well in the flour and pour in the yeast mixture. Gradually draw the flour into the yeast mixture, stirring until it forms a soft dough.

Turn the dough on to a floured surface and knead it for about 10 minutes or until it is smooth and elastic. Form the dough into a ball and roll it in a lightly oiled bowl. Cover the bowl with a damp cloth and leave it in a warm place until the dough has doubled in bulk.

Turn the dough on to a floured surface, punch it down and knead it lightly. Divide the dough into 6 pieces and roll each into a ball. Shape the balls, one at a time, into a flat tear-drop shape about 25 cm/10 inches long and 10 cm/4 inches wide, by stretching and patting the dough with your hands.

Arrange the shaped dough on lightly oiled baking sheets, cover with damp cloths and leave to rise for about 20 minutes.

Just before cooking, brush the centre of each *naan* with oil or water, leaving a dry margin about 1.5 cm/1/2 inch wide around the edge. Sprinkle the centre with onion seeds or chopped cashews.

Place the sheets, one at a time, under a very hot preheated grill (broiler). The *naan* should be about 7.5 cm/3 inches from the heat. Grill (broil) the *naan* for 2 to 3 minutes on each side or until cooked through and lightly browned. Serve immediately.
**Makes 6**

# Bulgarian Cheese Pastries

| METRIC/IMPERIAL | AMERICAN |
|---|---|
| *350 g/12 oz brynza or feta cheese* | *¾ lb brynza or feta cheese* |
| *4 tablespoons natural yogurt* | *¼ cup unflavored yogurt* |
| *2 egg yolks* | *2 egg yolks* |
| *1 egg white* | *1 egg white* |
| *freshly ground black pepper to taste* | *freshly ground black pepper to taste* |
| *175 g/6 oz butter, melted* | *¾ cup melted butter* |
| *12 sheets of filo or strudel pastry* | *12 sheets of filo or strudel pastry* |

Crumble the cheese and rub it through a sieve (strainer). Add the yogurt, egg yolks and white and beat the mixture to a smooth paste. Season it to taste with freshly ground black pepper. Transfer this filling to a large piping (pastry) bag fitted with a plain nozzle about 1 cm/⅓ inch diameter.

Prepare two heavy baking sheets by brushing them generously with melted butter.

To assemble each cheese pastry, place a sheet of pastry on a clean cloth and brush it with about 1 teaspoon of melted butter. Fold the sheet double, joining the long edges and brush the top surface with melted butter. Pipe a line of cheese filling along one long side of the pastry rectangle, leaving a 1.5 cm/½ inch space at each end. Using the cloth to lift the edge, roll up the pastry, starting on the filling side, into a cylinder. Brush it with butter and curl the ends in opposite directions to make a neat S-shaped spiral. Transfer the pastry carefully to the baking sheet.

When all the pastries have been shaped, bake them in a preheated, moderately hot oven (200°C/400°F, Gas Mark 6) for about 20 minutes, or until they are golden brown. Arrange the pastries on a heated dish and serve immediately.

**Makes 12**

# Orange Tart

Make sure the oranges for the decoration of this tart are thin skinned, or else peel them before slicing.

| METRIC/IMPERIAL | AMERICAN |
|---|---|
| *1 recipe rich shortcrust pastry* | *1 recipe enriched basic pie dough* |
| *(see page 83)* | *(see page 83)* |
| *50 g/2 oz unsalted butter* | *¼ cup sweet butter* |
| *4 tablespoons plain flour* | *¼ cup all-purpose flour* |
| *300 ml/½ pint milk* | *1¼ cups milk* |
| *150 ml/¼ pint natural yogurt* | *⅔ cup unflavored yogurt* |
| *50 g/2 oz soft brown sugar* | *¼ cup light brown sugar* |
| *juice and finely grated rind of* | *juice and finely grated rind of* |
| *1 orange* | *1 orange* |
| *1 tablespoon orange flower water* | *1 tablespoon orange flower water* |
| *(optional)* | *(optional)* |
| **To Decorate:** | **To Decorate:** |
| *3 small oranges, sliced* | *3 small oranges, sliced* |
| *100 g/4 oz granulated sugar* | *½ cup sugar* |
| *4 tablespoons fresh orange juice* | *¼ cup fresh orange juice* |

Lightly grease a 25 cm/10 inch pie tin or ring. Roll out the pastry thinly and leave it to rest for 10 minutes before lifting on the rolling pin and laying it on the tin. Ease the pastry gently into shape, trim the edges and chill for about 10 minutes.

Just before baking the pastry shell, line it with greaseproof (wax) paper or foil and weight it with rice or baking beans. Bake, on a baking sheet, in a preheated moderately hot oven (200°C/400°F, Gas Mark 6) for 10 minutes.

Take the sheet from the oven, remove the weights and lining paper. Lower the heat to moderate (180°C/350°F, Gas Mark 4) and bake for another 10 to 15 minutes, or until golden brown. Cool the pastry shell at room temperature to prevent it hardening.

Melt the butter in a saucepan and stir in the flour. Cook the *roux* for a minute or two without allowing it to colour, then gradually add the milk, stirring constantly, to form a thick sauce. Stir in the yogurt, sugar, orange rind and juice, and orange flower water. Cook for a few minutes more. Pour the filling into the cooled pastry case and set aside until cold. Arrange the sliced oranges over the filling.

Put the sugar and orange juice in a small saucepan and heat gently until the sugar has dissolved. Raise the heat and boil briskly until the syrup thickens and begins to turn colour. Immediately pour the glaze over the tart. Chill well before serving.
**Serves 6-8**

ORANGE TART AND CHOCOLATE CAKE *(page 90)*

# Chocolate Cake

METRIC/IMPERIAL
100 g/4 oz dark chocolate
150 ml/¼ pint boiling water
275 g/10 oz plain flour
¾ teaspoon baking powder
1½ teaspoons bicarbonate of soda
175 g/6 oz butter
275 g/10 oz soft brown sugar
3 large eggs
150 ml/¼ pint natural yogurt
1 teaspoon vanilla essence
4 tablespoons sieved apricot jam
   for filling
**For the icing:**
175 g/6 oz unsalted butter
350 g/12 oz icing sugar
6 tablespoons cocoa powder
1-2 tablespoons strong black coffee
   or orange juice

AMERICAN
4 squares semi-sweet chocolate
⅔ cup boiling water
2½ cups all-purpose flour
¾ teaspoon baking powder
1½ teaspoons baking soda
¾ cup butter
1½ cups light brown sugar
3 large eggs
⅔ cup unflavored yogurt
1 teaspoon vanilla extract
¼ cup strained apricot jam,
   for filling
**For the frosting:**
¾ cup sweet butter
2½ cups confectioners' sugar
6 tablespoons unsweetened cocoa
   powder
1-2 tablespoons strong black coffee
   or orange juice

Break up the chocolate and pour boiling water over it. Stir until smooth and set aside to cool a little. Sift together the flour, baking powder and soda.

Cream the butter in a large bowl, add the sugar and beat until the mixture is light and fluffy. Beat in the eggs, one at a time, adding a spoonful of the flour mixture with each addition. Pour in the melted chocolate and beat until well blended. Beat in the remaining flour, and the yogurt and vanilla.

Divide the mixture between two greased 23 cm/9 inch sandwich tins (layer cake pans) and bake in a preheated moderate oven (180°C/350°F, Gas Mark 4) for about 35 minutes, or until well risen and springy to touch. Turn the cakes out and cool on a wire rack.

Sandwich the cakes together with sieved (strained) apricot jam.

To make the butter icing (frosting) cream the butter. Sift the icing (confectioners') sugar and cocoa together and gradually add to the butter beating to a stiff cream. Add enough coffee or orange juice to produce a working consistency.

Spread the icing (frosting) over the top and sides of the cake and pull it into irregular peaks with the tip of a round bladed knife.

Store the finished cake in an airtight box or tin for at least 24 hours before cutting it.
**Serves 8-10**

# INDEX

## Acknowledgments

The authors would like
to thank Rye Tiles and
Robert Payne Antiques.

PDO 79/548